Praise for *Wild and Free*

Wild and Free is equal parts encouragement and challenge to live the wild and free lives our heavenly Father has planned for us. Through Jess Connolly and Hayley Morgan's open and honest writing, I felt like I've gotten to know them better, to know myself better, and most importantly to know the loving God I serve better! Read it for yourself and for your daughters.

Korie Robertson, Duck Dynasty and
author of *Strong and Kind*

Imagine living in the moment with God, defined by His truth, without the weight of shame, fear, insecurities, or expectations of others. It's not too far out of reach! Page by page, Jess Connolly and Hayley Morgan are the friends who take your hand and transparently lead you to that beautiful place with the Lord. Every woman needs to read *Wild and Free*!

Lysa TerKeurst, *New York Times* bestselling author
and president of Proverbs 31 Ministries

I tend to play it safe, hesitate, and shy away from becoming all God created me to be. With the passionate voice of two visionaries and the beautiful blend of gut-honest truth shared from their own stories and struggles, Jess Connolly and Hayley Morgan have written a message every woman needs to read.

Renee Swope, author of *A Confident Heart* and
Proverbs 31 Ministries radio cohost

As a woman who sometimes doesn't believe it's actually possible to live wild and free, this book is water to my soul. Jess Connolly and Hayley Morgan's words are full of grace and truth as they remind us that being wild and free is actually how we were always created to be.

Jamie Ivey, podcast host of
The Happy Hour with Jamie Ivey

Wild and Free is a breath of fresh air. Jess Connolly and Hayley Morgan share their hearts and their story with refreshing candor, vulnerability, and grace. I love them. I love this book, and I know you will too.

Alli Worthington, author of *Breaking Busy: How to
Find Peace and Purpose in a World of Crazy*

Wild and Free is the missing puzzle piece for anyone who has ever felt like they are stifling a rebellious streak, crazy whim, or creative idea. This book promises to point those urges in God's direction and will bolster your confidence to help you live out your hidden purpose.

Whitney English, founder and
creator of Day Designer

Wild and *free* are two of my favorite words, and now there's a book that explores both in a way that is practical, applicable, and relatable. I love how Jess Connolly and Hayley Morgan dig deep into not only the *how* but also the *why* behind each word! Each chapter will make you feel inspired and encouraged to pursue both, not just in principle, but in practice.

Bianca Juarez Olthoff, writer, teacher,
and chief storyteller for A21

Into the milieu of self-help, "do more, try harder" books and Facebook, Instagram, and Pinterest pressures, Jess Connolly and Hayley Morgan have given a sweet gift to the women of their generation—freedom from finding our identity in anything aside from the love of our heavenly Father and the work of Jesus Christ. With refreshing transparency and deep devotion, they respond to the pressures women experience today with answers that are anything but trite religiosity. Because we are loved by God, we can live in freedom and find a place of rest as He grows us into all He has for us. I'm honored to recommend their fine work.

Elyse M. Fitzpatrick, author of
Good News for Weary Women

Open these pages only if you are ready for your life to be radically changed. Jess Connolly and Hayley Morgan have penned an important message of grace and truth for women, freeing them from the chains of misplaced identity. Like a conversation with two wise friends, *Wild and Free* is refreshing balm for weary souls like mine. I laughed, cried, and danced in celebration as I devoured these nourishing words! I'm grabbing extra copies for my daughters to read when they are older. This book will no doubt change generations as women walk alongside Jess and Hayley, uncovering the truth that in Christ alone, we are free.

Lara Casey, author of *Make It Happen*

If you feel small and scared, constantly worried about pleasing God or finding his good plans for your life, then I have good news! *Wild and Free* is the key to unlocking that cage of anxiety and flying straight into the freedom Christ died to give you.

Susie Davis, author of *Unafraid* and cofounder
of Austin Christian Fellowship

Wild and Free touches the deepest parts of a woman's heart, giving her permission to both live with abandon and shed the shackles of doubt and unworthiness. Jess Connolly and Hayley Morgan's friendship is felt with the turn of each page and reminds us we're not alone. In fact, their relationship reminds us we're part of a beautiful community of women who desperately want to love big and live unapologetically meaningful lives—wild and free.

Emily Ley, creative director of Emily Ley Paper
& Gifts and author of *Grace Not Perfection*

Jess Connolly and Hayley Morgan have given you the key to unlock the dungeon of performance and perfectionism. Read this book and watch the chains fall off—and then come outside and rest in the warmth of God's great love.

Jessica Thompson, author and speaker

What Jess Connolly and Hayley Morgan have done here is a beautiful work. It reflects not only the truth of the gospel, but also the truth of who they each are and how uniquely God has made us. I'm thankful for the way *Wild and Free* gave me permission to be me and to love others the way Christ does.

Annie F. Downs, author of *Looking for Lovely*
and *Let's All Be Brave*

Where social jockeying is the norm and self-worth is measured in clicks, our hearts are in exile. Where *do* I fit? And can this world even handle me? Jess Connolly and Hayley Morgan's words are gospel-soaked arrows of hope shot through the desert noise. As it turns out, the opposite of lost is free.

Shannan Martin, author of *Falling Free*
(available fall 2016)

If ever there was a time for a book about how freedom in Christ directly speaks to womanhood in our demanding culture, it is now. No matter what our particular calling as women, we are enough! But goodness, I needed this truth in this way from women who are struggling to figure it out, just like I am.

Jami Nato, blogger/writer/speaker

Jess Connolly and Hayley Morgan are a dream team role model duo for young women everywhere. Their minds, souls, and spirits are wildly different, but together, their hearts gracefully point to one common purpose: to find freedom and rest in God alone.

Erin Loechner, author of *Chasing Slow*
(forthcoming), *Design for Mankind* blog

In a culture where we are constantly bombarded with the message to fit in and conform, *Wild and Free* is a desperately needed call to action, summoning the passions, desires, and dreams that have, for far too long, been hidden in the caverns of our hearts. Jess Connolly and Hayley Morgan have somehow managed to unpack our Christian boxes and ideologies, leaving us with the freedom— God's freedom—to run wildly in the direction of the call of God in each of our lives.

Kennesha Buycks, inspirational speaker
and writer, *Restoration House* blog

Wild and Free

A HOPE-FILLED ANTHEM FOR THE WOMAN WHO FEELS SHE IS BOTH TOO MUCH AND NEVER ENOUGH

JESS CONNOLLY AND HAYLEY MORGAN

ZONDERVAN

Wild and Free
Copyright © 2016 by Jessica Ashleigh Connolly and Hayley E. Morgan

Requests for information should be addressed to:
Zondervan, 3900 Sparks Dr. SE, Grand Rapids, Michigan 49546

ISBN 978-0-310-34554-1 (ebook)

Library of Congress Cataloging-in-Publication Data

Names: Connolly, Jess, author.
Title: Wild and free : a hope-filled anthem for the woman who feels she is both too
    much and never enough / Jess Connolly and Hayley Morgan.
Description: Grand Rapids: Zondervan, 2016 | Includes bibliographical references.
Identifiers: LCCN 2015045430 | ISBN 9780310345534 (softcover)
Subjects: LCSH: Christian women—Religious life.
Classification: LCC BV4527.C644 2016 | DCC 248.8/43—dc23 LC record available at
    http://lcnn.loc.gov/2015045430

Published in association with literary agent Jenni Burke of D. C. Jacobson & Associates
LLC, an Author Management Company www.dcjacobson.com

Cover design: Juicebox Designs
Cover Photo: Getty Images
Interior design: Kait Lamphere

First Printing February 2016 / Printed in the United States of America

This is for you.
You are already enough
and never, ever too much.

Contents

Foreword

First, I like you already that you would pick up this book, written by two people I adore and titled with two words I am so terribly moved by. Because you have this book in hand, I imagine we would be kindred friends.

Wild and *free*. While I love these two words, for most of my life, I would have heard them with an ache of insufficiency inside. I was the girl who always feared she was too much for a room, so I stuffed myself into a presentable, appropriate package. Yet I was exploding—exploding with passion and gifts and vision and opinions and leadership.

Maybe you are too.

I remember having this image in my mind that heaven would be the place I would finally feel free, like a horse without lead ropes and fences and bridles. I just couldn't imagine I would ever feel that freedom in this life, not with all the roles and expectations that surrounded me.

Oh, the lies we choose to believe in the name of humility and holiness.

God designed us for adventure because He knew following Him would be one. I am blessed to meet women around the world, and I believe this wild and free faith is growing in us. It isn't wild in rebellion; it is wild in obedience. And it isn't free to do whatever we want; it is free to do whatever He calls us to do. This kind of faith is powerful, and it is beautiful.

As it turns out, you can experience God's wild freedom in this life, as I have discovered over the past five years. Freedom began for me the moment I began to fear God more than people, and as that transformation has happened, God has been going wild all around me. He began leading me toward more and more risky places and asking me to step out in faith. And here is what I can say as I have closed my eyes and with so much fear, and took the leap anyway:

Risking for God is the greatest choice you will ever make.

Robert Frost's "The Road Not Taken" is one of the only works I can still recite after two decades out of school. I have always been drawn to that overgrown path in the wilderness, even though it scares me a little even now. Truth is, while I wish I were a more confident, rebellious pioneer, God has had to nearly force me to the wild new paths He has for me and for the ministry I lead.

I would never have imagined the places He would take me, but trust me, I would never want to miss them. You don't either.

I am compelled to call as many of you as possible to the roads less traveled. There are so many living in bondage, and we are called to be free and set others free, because this is what Christ has done for us! We are called to take the wild road, the adventurous road, and to risk big for the glory of our God and the good of the people we love.

If you feel held back, this book will spark something. If you feel that ache I have felt for freedom, prepare to encounter it in a big way—the kind of way in which there is no turning back.

Jess and Hayley are not only excellent writers; they also have a deep passionate vision and hope for you to be wild and free. They have fought for themselves, and now that they have tasted life with this wild, free faith, they want you to have it too.

These pages will show you just how much you are loved, how much you've been fought for, and what it truly means when we read in God's Word, "It is for freedom that Christ set you free!" (Galatians 5:1).

Jennie Allen

Introduction // Jess and Hayley

In many ways, we couldn't be more alike and more different all at once.

The first time we officially met in the flesh, we crowded our six kids—each of us had three at the time—into a local café. Jess and her family had just moved to the state of Indiana, and Hayley had invited the Connollys to come for a visit. We'd talked online and communicated as bloggers, watching one another and interacting with each other's lives online. We had a few mutual "real life" friends, so it felt totally normal to pack the kids into the car and drive a few hours to make the relationship a proper one. That day wasn't monumental, and we didn't exchange "best friend" bracelets—but it was a sweet promise of what more the Lord would do in our lives, through one another, in the future.

A few weeks later, we were chatting on the phone, still relative strangers, and together we had kind of a crazy, wild-eyed idea: Should we plan a conference together? Gather a bunch of women under the banner of the gospel and the idea that *they* have influence? It seemed right to us, and, thankfully, the Holy Spirit blinded us to all that could go wrong and to fully comprehending what a large ministry we were beginning.

Our friendship became more intimate, and our interaction turned to walking together daily. As the time of the conference grew closer and the Lord was refining us for the task at hand, we exchanged dozens, even hundreds of texts a day. We FaceTimed, Skyped, and drove to see one another as often as we could—even after Jess moved from Indiana back to South Carolina. And it wasn't just work and conference details that we were constantly discussing—we were sharing our hearts and fears, simultaneously walking through some of the very same trials and blessings of being newish leaders and business owners, and both adding new babies to the mix.

The Influence Conference happened in 2012, and then we launched The Influence Network on January 1, 2013—fourteen days before Hayley welcomed her fourth baby and twenty-eight days before Jess had her fourth as well. We were plowing ahead and trying to acclimate as quickly as possible to this new season that both of us suddenly found ourselves in. We grew together over the next months, and that's when the phrase "wild and free" started popping up repeatedly in our conversations.

Something about ministering to others can really bring out your inner brokenness, amen? And ministering so closely alongside someone else can be an incredible blessing, as well as a pretty hilarious study in human nature. Because of our wildly different pasts, stories, and personalities, we responded to some trials, blessings, and pitfalls incredibly differently. There were times when Jess would get angry, mouthy, and frustrated, while Hayley's proclivity would be to shrink away, avoid conflict, and get quiet. We would preach "wild and free" to one another to combat our natural and sin-filled responses, but the phrase meant vastly different things to each of us—though the Lord and His redemption meant the same.

As God continued to knit our hearts together, we found that our base insecurities and the ways we responded to the world were also contrasting. Hayley hated for anyone to be disappointed in her—essentially being told she wasn't enough or hadn't done enough. Jess lived with an underlying fear of being too much for the people around her. But we both knew what it was like to flip back and forth between those insecurities and concerns.

And the way we loved women and encouraged them? That

was different too. When Hayley spoke, she was like a loving, sweet mama reminding everyone of their worth and identity, encouraging them not to toil or spin, reminding them how valuable rest and abiding are for us. Jess was the gal who wanted to charge hell with a handgun, who wanted to ride into battle and call women to arms. We were like two sides of a coin.

Hayley spoke rest, gentleness, and freedom, while Jess tended to proclaim wild action, response, and hope.

And one day in October, about a year and a half after that phone call where we decided to start a conference, we had another wild idea over the phone. Maybe this declaration of "wild and free" was meant for more than just us to trade back and forth? Maybe it was a book we should write together? The more we prayed and talked, the more we realized: It was a book we could *only* write together. It needed both voices and both perspectives. It needed Jess's "let's do this!" coaching call from the sidelines, and it needed Hayley's "there, there" comfort and reminder to abide.

We watched and listened, and we realized that so many of you feel the same way we do. You feel like you're too much or you're never enough, or both all at once. You aren't sure who exactly you're supposed to be as a daughter of God and a part of this kingdom. You feel timid, defensive, and bruised, but you also feel ready. And we feel all those things along with you.

As we started to pull the string of "wild and free," we found that both of those characteristics were accessible to us because our Creator embodies them both. And that left us with an even bigger question: If God is wild and if God is free, what does that mean for us? The answer we've landed on is that we believe we have the liberty to walk out our own wild freedom in pursuit of His kingdom, and He will help us as we go. He is the one who calls us to be wild—walking in who God created us to be. And He is the one who calls us to be free—resting in what Jesus has done for us.

This book is our love letter to you. We believe Jesus is mighty in you and His grace is overwhelming, covering all your insecurities and fears and hurts and what-ifs. It's not that we believe you should be more wild and free; we believe you already are and might just need the encouragement to live it out.

From the heart of two friends to many new friends:

We're praying for you and we love you. Let's live wild and free.

The Anthem of *Wild and Free*

The world may tell us we're too much and never enough.
But we can walk wildly in who God created us to be
and rest freely in the work Jesus did for us.
We do not have to be confined or conformed by cultural expectations.
We are unchained from our past and unafraid of our future.
We choose compassion over comparison.
We love without condition, without reserve.
Our eyes are on God; we hold nothing back;
we run fast and strong; we do not hide our light.
We aren't wild and free for our sake alone;
rather we sing life, hope, and truth over the world
with abandon—just as our God sings over us.
We are wild and free.
And we are poised to do mighty things, in Christ alone.

We Have Become Tame and Tethered

It was a normal Tuesday afternoon—my toddler had just gone down for a nap, and the big kids were coming home from school soon, giving me a moment to catch my breath. The sun was squinting past the shades, creeping across the floor as I sat there restless and exhausted, craving escape. My day had been flat and seemingly pointless, and I was feeling frustrated about how all of life tends to be overflowing with maintenance and monotony. A wave of wanting more washed over me, leaving my soul pricked.

I wonder if you have those flashes too. On your sofa or at the coffee shop, in bed or in the carpool line, when suddenly you're aware of just how tame this life feels, how tediously the same it always is—day after day.

On that particular Tuesday, I was looking for something to watch on TV to add a little levity to the day that wouldn't also corrode my brain and soul. You know the feeling? When all your heart really needs is a happy medium between the local news and the trashy reality TV show? As I sat flipping and searching, there it was. Typically, such a program might bore me or barely register, but on this day, when I felt very aware of the entrapment of the mundane, it captured me. There on the screen, I saw horses, and my spirit did a flip.

It was a documentary on the wild horses of the Outer Banks. Fascinating footage filled the screen, burning this fiercely stunning picture in my mind. Beautiful, wild mustangs running in slow motion, kicking up sand, letting the sun dance over their beautiful, messy manes.

I grew up just hours away from the Outer Banks of North Carolina, but I never knew anything about this phenomenon. I went on to learn that these horses are the direct descendants of the Spanish mustangs that came with the earliest European explorers to the North Carolina coast. What's more, the breed remains completely and utterly wild, roaming free over twelve thousand acres of beaches that make up the Outer Banks.

But my awe and admiration of these wild things quickly turned to shock. I was jarred by the stark contrast to my world when I saw those animals in the wild. I sat—that day, and now—in a carefully curated home, surrounded by things I'd collected in an attempt to build a habitat. From where I rested in the vintage club chair that had been a miraculous find at Goodwill two years before, I could see my small but overflowing life. There were stacks and piles and shelves of books, filled with knowledge and the help I so desperately believed I needed. My kitchen utensil drawer was filled to overflowing with odds and ends—a garlic press I'd used only once and three different black plastic slotted spoons I'd procured over the years. Papers upon papers upon papers from my kids' school littered my desk—picture forms, snack schedules, weekly updates. I looked around at all the things that felt necessary to survive in my world, but those same things seemed superfluous when I saw a wild mustang sprinting freely on a sandy North Carolina beach.

I am struck by the thought that the female mustang doesn't need a manual on how to find fresh water or a thirty-page PDF on feeding her colts. There is no formal council or schedule determining how she needs to be in community with her herd. I see no books lying around the sand dunes proclaiming three easy steps for her to *Be the Horse That Has It All.* She knows exactly who she is without being told. She's not caught up in the trappings of the world, because she is wild.

Women in the Wild

I've spent a lot of my adult life thinking about the original wild woman, our girl Eve. I think about her eating that fruit and how I probably would have done it too. I think about sin and how it affects me, and about the way our world is now so fallen. But occasionally I want to get lost pondering the minutes, hours, and days that occurred just before that disastrous bite.

It all started here:

> And the rib that the LORD God had taken from the man he made into a woman and brought her to the man. Then the man said,
>
>> "This at last is bone of my bones
>>   and flesh of my flesh;
>> she shall be called Woman,
>>   because she was taken out of Man."
>
> Therefore a man shall leave his father and his mother and hold fast to his wife, and they shall become one flesh. And the man and his wife were both naked and were not ashamed.
>
> *Genesis 2:22–25 ESV*

Oh goodness, I want to know about Eve! What was she like? How did she walk? I wish we had three chapters between the creation of Eve and the point when it all went downhill. Did she like to run through the garden and smell the flowers? Did she cuddle with the animals or make paint out of berries? And how did she talk to her Creator? How did she wake up, and what was the look on her face when she caught a reflection of herself in the waters that covered the earth? Can I confess? It is nearly impossible for me to picture her naked *and* unashamed. Let's face it. We live in a world filled with heavy under-eye concealer, Spanx, and teeth whitening on the regular.

I picture Eve being just like that mustang. I imagine that she lived in a very pure and wild state, secure in who she was and confident in her purpose. I imagine her looking God full in the face, smiling because she knows she is right where she was always meant to be. In my mind's eye, she laughs with Adam, and she isn't afraid to ask questions since everything is so new and she is so incredibly safe. I like to picture her being imaginative and creative, seeing beauty in creation, and being wildly resourceful with what she's been given.

It's fun to picture, but it's all just imagining, since we don't really know. What we do know is that for a time, she was in perfect communion with her heavenly Father. She was in perfect communion with *our* heavenly Father, just like we will be someday in eternity. I like to think about her during that short period of paradise, because she is our prototype. Eve is our girl. She was the original forerunner of "wild and free," the mother of the daughters of God.

There is one overwhelming similarity between Eve and those horses on the beach that I can't seem to shake. Both live out of the reality that their identity and purpose are uncomplicated and unhindered by their own insecurity or need for acknowledgment. They were created, cared for, and set free to do what they were made to do. Born wild, neither Eve nor the horses ever questioned how to do it or whether they were the right ones for the job—they simply moved forward with purpose in the roles set forth before them.

And here in the trappings of domesticated life, I ache so deeply for what they have. That day when I first saw the horses running wild, I couldn't relate to that unbridled and unshackled freedom. But oh, I wanted it.

Maybe that's you too. Maybe you don't picture yourself like a wild mustang running down the beach, free from burden or obligation. Maybe you feel burdened by the phone that always sits so near to you, the meetings that never seem to stop, the list that only grows and yells louder each day. Maybe you don't feel free in your relationships with God or others, but instead feel stifled inside of yourself and your connections. Maybe answering the call to live wild and free sounds amazing—if only you knew how. If only you had the time.

I'm afraid we're missing out on transcendent abundance by ignoring this call. What if we already have everything in us necessary to move forward wild and free, and we just don't know it?

The Burden We Carry

For Eve, the wild identity she was able to run with was short-lived. It was the very questioning of the power of her identity that ultimately led to her downfall. And as women today, it seems we're still there—born into the tension of the culture war created by Eve. We can only imagine what it would be like to feel safe and wild all at once, when our current reality leaves us feeling anything but.

To say the burden on women in our current culture is heavy is a vast understatement. We live under the national assumption that women should look impeccable at all times—regardless of age. Not only that, but women are expected to have glittering personalities on the inside, all the while being strong and successful and self-sufficient.

As if the crushing weight of impossible expectations weren't enough, the situation is only made more precarious because the expectations change drastically from city to city, community to community, even person to person.

Some women are expected to work and build careers—but only the kind that their community deems meaningful. Some women would be corrected for having career ambitions and are encouraged to stay home, caring for children and having dinner ready by five. Some of you feel like you're not up to par because you don't make amazing, home-baked treats and goodies for your kids, while still others would be shunned for feeding their children refined sugar.

Personally, I've felt the whiplash of moving from community to community and knowing instantly I didn't measure up or fit in. I had worked and strived to fit the proper definition of womanhood where I'd just come from and then had the breath knocked out of me by the staggering rejection from not fitting into the next place.

Our problem isn't one caused by our mothers or the mothers that came before them; it's a tension of biblical proportions exacerbated by the enemy of our Creator. The truth remains that we were brought forth in the midst of a battle regarding our worth, purpose, and our assumed role in this life. At first glance, the battle lines seem clear, but in reality the voices and messages are complicated at best. The confusion lies in the deception that began with Eve's partaking of the shiny, beautiful fruit because someone told her that was best for her.

That deception is still active today. From one camp we hear that we are to walk in a straight line—be seen and not heard, not disturbing anyone with our thoughts, dreams, voices, or gifts the Father gave us. Swinging to the opposite extreme is a vocal group insisting we must stand up and take control—get what is ours, forcefully find our own place, and make our own way, at the cost of anyone and anything that stands in our way. And of course, there are all sorts of tensions, questions, and limitations in between.

Do you see it? Inside your friend groups and the halls where you worship? Can you feel the burden of expectation, of what women are "supposed" to be? Mantles have been placed on us that genuinely aren't rooted in Scripture, and they are slowing us down.

Ladies, this is what scares me. When a horse is finally tamed and trained, bearing the burden of saddle and human expectations alike, she is called broken. It is only then that she performs the duties expected of her.

I don't know about you, but I don't think that's what God ever had in mind for Eve. And I don't think that's what God ever had in mind for you and me. In the Bible, He speaks of yokes and submission, and there are commandments and thousands of pieces of wisdom, yes. But His authoritative mission in our lives has *never* been to break our spirits; it's geared to set them free to give Him as much glory as possible.

But sometimes His gentle voice is drowned out by the demanding ones in our physical lives, the comments and commands of those telling us who or how to be.

I see women believing and repeating the lie that motherhood is the highest calling for all women. Did you know that's nowhere in the Bible? The only reference to a chief call on anyone's life is found in Matthew 6:33: Seek first the Father's kingdom and His righteousness. We watch as that lie discourages those who are unable to be mothers and immobilizes those who love their children and still feel called to serve in other contexts. I see broken women believing the only role for them is quiet service and the only pace is nonstop. They exhaust themselves as they serve out of obligation, not worship. I see women believing it's brash and wrong to seek the wisdom of God, waiting on others to intercede and teach them the Word rather than seeking first the kingdom themselves.

Outside the church, we have just as many loud and confounding voices telling us who to be. Pop stars and media moguls shape culture with lean bodies and tight and exposed skin. Now that celebrities have social media, we're provided with an ever-present portal into their worlds, constantly reminding us how much better they have it and how wonderful it all is. All of our excuses to not live an incredibly beautiful life are dissipating. Pinterest provides us with a prescription to live big, well, loud, tidy, and—ultimately—perfectly put together. This shiny, make-believe life we are chasing perpetuates the myth that everyone else's perception of us is ultimately our reality.

The point is that no matter where our gaze is right now, we're trapped by expectation, and it seems like we're destined to fail. Our eyes dart from habitat to habitat, wondering what is wrong with us and looking for ways we can become more like the perfect woman, whoever she is.

But there is a way back. There is a way home. In our lifetimes, we probably won't return to the Garden of Eden to all live there peacefully together, but by looking more closely at our good God, we can drown out the noise and hear a little more clearly.

Treasures, Not Tools

It's terribly sad that here in America, we've turned the phrase "daddy issues" into a joke. For so many women, this is where the brokenness begins.

My biological father is a hilarious and fun-loving teacher; he's the kind of guy who lights up a room, and no one tells a story better than him. The hard part is that for most of my life, he's been an overseas teacher. Starting when I was around three, the bulk of my relationship with him has been built in over-the-phone snippets and once- or twice-yearly visits. I have a handful of sweet memories from growing up with him, and we're making as many as we can now, but I have many more of him absent than I do of him present. The hole and ache this left in my heart felt ever-present throughout childhood. I constantly missed my dad, and I consistently wondered why I wasn't good enough for him to stay.

As an adult, I can look back on that time and say, "This wasn't about you! It wasn't because you were broken or not enough!" But it's hard to tell a three-year-old heart that. As an adult, I'm learning to process the truth that the decisions my earthly dad made weren't based on how much or how little he loved me. He loved me and my sister so much—and still does—and his life choices weren't about us. We're learning to find our footing and figure out what our relationship looks like, living on two different continents. Moreover, I'm learning to apply the truth that my heavenly Father is working all things together for the good of those who love Him.

My stepfather walked into our life when I was in late elementary school, and he began the arduous task of learning to love and shepherd my older sister and me. By that time in our young lives, we were rambunctious and more than a little unruly, prone to getting into all kinds of trouble and experts at fighting with my mom. I made his job hard because I lied and disobeyed incessantly as a teenager, but also because my heart was already so hard and closed by the time he made his entrance.

In hurt and confusion, my young heart had already made a conclusion based on lies the enemy told me: Men see women as tools, not as treasure. I assumed that all men saw women as the people to make dinner, look pretty, and generally help men as second-class citizens. I decided the whole father-daughter thing was a sham. It wasn't real. Everyone was just pretending. And as my own fathers tried to love me, I allowed myself only to go through the motions of those relationships—not needing anything, not expecting anything, finding affirmation and acceptance in other places since surely that father love could not be real or sturdy or dependable.

As I grew up and saw my friends confide in their fathers, casually sit on their laps, or even dance together at weddings, a part of me felt bad for them. I assumed they'd been duped as well, tricked into believing the men in their lives actually wanted good for them. I knew the real truth—the protection of fathers was really just overbearing control, the affection they gave was only about receiving affirmation in return, and mostly these fathers spent their days thinking about their own lives and dreams and goals, with daughters merely serving as decoration.

It's not just my story or my mistaken understanding, unfortunately. I think we have a generation filled with women who have incredibly twisted ideals of what it means to be a daughter. They've been abused, forgotten, put down, used. And in the process, maybe, like me, you've picked up a false understanding of what it means to be a daughter of God.

I pray my story isn't familiar, but I know for many of you it's far too familiar or even incredibly tame compared to what you've encountered. Some of you were raised in blessed and peaceful homes, and your picture of a father has been left mostly unscathed. For that I am so grateful. I pray the same for my daughter. And yet, for all of us, it's still pretty inescapable. At some point, in some way, men (fathers or otherwise) *will* affect our view of God—for better and for worse.

Statistically, the lack of or abuse by a father figure is incredibly evident. We know that between 66 and 90 percent of women in the sex industry were sexually abused as children.[1] We know that more women are employed in the sex industry right now than at any other time in history.[2] A staggering 90 percent of homeless and runaway children are from fatherless homes.[3] Sixty-three percent of teenage suicide attempts occur inside homes without father figures.[4] Seventy-one percent of high school dropouts and 85 percent of youths in prison come from single-parent, fatherless homes.[5]

We see the widespread effect of this cultural injury everywhere we turn. And we often end up living as though we are tools instead of believing that God has called us His treasure: "See what great love the Father has lavished on us, that we should be called children of God! And that is what we are!" (1 John 3:1).

I genuinely believe we can spend an infinite number of hours in counseling, create hundreds of rehabilitation programs for abused and battered little girls, and champion single moms till we're blue in the face—but we will still be lost if we do not point a generation of women to the truth.

And the truth, dear friends, is this: Our standing has never wavered with our Father. Though the world has twisted what it means to be a daughter, His stance and His position toward us has absolutely stayed resolute. The world cannot dictate what it means to be treasured by our Father, but the love and relationship of our heavenly Father can heal and transcend the damage done here on earth.

The Creator of the universe didn't just love and speak us into being, He also called us *good*—the same word He called the massive, majestic oceans and the sun that lights our solar system and keeps us all sustained. He sent His Son to make a way for us while we were still broken and sinful and sitting with our fingers in our ears, unwilling to hear truth. His Holy Spirit runs wild in our lives, guiding us, leading us, growing us, and groaning for us so we can genuinely be in community with Him. We mean the world to Him—not because we're good or we've earned it, but because we are His treasure, the apple of His eye, the daughters He is coming back for. He has never seen us as a tool. We have always been the prize worth fighting for.

The Lord began to drastically heal my perception of being a daughter once I had my own. Gloriana Eloise Connolly was born on March 14, 2008, and from my perspective, I've never seen another little lady be so loved by a daddy. Watching my husband, Nick, with our girl has been so restorative because his ability to genuinely love her is because of the way he has been so genuinely loved by our God. When she is disobedient, when she runs from him, when she wants her own way—he loves her all the same. Before she did anything good, before she was useful in any way, shape, or form, when she was only needy and not at all helpful in the slightest—he loved her and would have given his life for her. If my sinful and broken husband can love a daughter so well and so fiercely, how much more can a perfect and holy God love us?

Ambassadors, Not Orphans

Our story as daughters doesn't stop at our adoption into the family of God that was purchased by the blood of Jesus. God didn't just make a way for us to go back home; He also called us into His kingdom. I see so many women stop here, at this point in their relationship with Him. It's almost as if they say, "OK! They let my poor orphan self into the family. Now I'll work to pay for my spot at the table and try not to make a fuss."

This is where I see women feeling very much *allowed* in the kingdom but still quite unsure of where they're supposed to go and what they're supposed to do. But check this out. Second Corinthians 5:20 reads, "We are therefore Christ's ambassadors, as though God were making his appeal through us. We implore you on Christ's behalf: Be reconciled to God."

If we are truly God's ambassadors, we're like the people from other countries riding around in long limos with the little waving flags, stopping traffic all day. We have been given great authority through Christ! We're called to action! And that passage says it's as if God is making His appeal through us! Ladies, you are not called to sit on your hands in silence. You are called by our great God to run wild into our culture, calling out an incredible message of life: "God loves you! World! God loves you and made a way for you! Come with me! You don't have to live lost and alone! My Dad has a place for you! He sees you as His ultimate treasure!"

If we're being honest, this isn't always how we live. It's so easy to be unsure of our calling. We're fearful to step outside the lines that culture has drawn for us, determined not to say or do the wrong thing, until ultimately we feel as if we're saying or doing very little of importance. On the other hand, sometimes we feel silenced and so incredibly unheard when we do speak truth. And instead of living in the confidence that we've been commissioned as God's ambassadors, we become confused and disoriented in the face of others' expectations for us.

In light of our standing with God as adopted daughters and ambassadors, I feel compelled to tell you that I believe we've forgotten, starting with myself, that we already have a great High Priest. If we are indeed the holy nation and royal priesthood mentioned in 1 Peter 2:9, should there be a hierarchy of Christian celebrities who are seen as special, anointed, or more equipped to do the work of the gospel? The men and women on the stage, on the back of the books—they can certainly be guides, but they can never take the place of Jesus as the one who intercedes for us. If they do, our hopes are misplaced.

I go to conferences, and I see the beauty that can come from gleaning wisdom and hearing truth. But I also see the shift in my sisters' hearts when they put leaders on pedestals they just can't live on. Not only are they entrapping the leader they're learning from, ensuring that she'll let the world down when it turns out she's also a sinner, but they're also putting down their belief in God's wild and holy call on their own lives as daughters and ambassadors.

Born to Speak Boldly

If we are indeed a treasure, if we don't need priests to intercede for us, and if we're born to be wild and free, then this changes everything—including how we talk to God.

My daughter, Glory, comes down the stairs in the morning talking. She goes to sleep at night talking. On Saturdays, she's often the last to wake up, but she'll plod down the steps, words and plans and ideas spilling out of her mouth, completely oblivious to what is on TV or any conversation that may have been taking place. Without taking a breath, she'll keep talking and climb right into my husband's lap and nuzzle up to him, and the words will just keep coming out until she falls asleep at night.

She is a daughter who knows her standing. She is a daughter who knows that the lines of communication are always open. She loves to talk to her dad. She doesn't go through a middleman or ask her brothers to tell her what he's said. If she is confused, hurt, lonely, or scared, she goes right up to his lap and grabs his face and asks for his attention. Shoot, she'll kick a few shins to get there if need be.

And yet I see my sisters in Christ, and myself, walking in the most timid forms of communication with our loving and powerful Father. We say, "He doesn't want to talk to me like that," or "I don't hear from God when I read the Word." We beg our friends to pray for us before we ever think to pray for ourselves. Most of us talk and process and digest with others far more than we will turn our face to our Father and tell Him what is going on.

Ladies, we need not live lives of timid communication. When

Eve was in the garden and talking with God, no one called her presumptuous for talking to the King of the universe. No one smacked her hand for speaking out of turn. She walked in wild and free communication with the one love she'd always known; only back then, it wasn't considered wild—it was simply natural.

The problem is, sometimes when we walk in open and free communication with our Father, some will consider us dramatic, fake, emotional, false, and too much. And sometimes it is this very fear that holds us back from the true and beautiful intimacy God offers us. But it doesn't have to be this way. Just like Nick loves to talk to Glory, God loves to talk to us. He's here, and He's listening.

The Easy Comfort of the Tame Life

I think it's cool that minimalism is coming back into style. Have you heard all the excitement about the capsule wardrobe? Essentially the idea is that you pare down your wardrobe to thirty to fifty items that you really, really love, and you get rid of the rest. Not only do you get rid of the rest, but you don't keep purchasing. For a set amount of time, you keep those clothes and wear them intentionally and thoughtfully. Hayley was one of the first people to introduce this idea to me, and it works so well for her. She's a pioneer of minimalism.

But then there's me. Ladies, I'm not sure how to tell you this, but I'm awful at minimalism. For the first few years that I kept hearing about the capsule, I would flat-out tell people, "I don't want to do that." I like having too many things, and I love constantly adding things. I wouldn't say I'm an avid shopper, but the last thing I wanted taken away was my freedom to snag an eleven-dollar shirt from the clearance rack of Target when I pop in to buy diapers.

I avoided the whole idea until I really felt conviction stirring in my belly. Essentially, the more I surrounded myself with women who were passionate leaders and worshipers of God, the more I realized they lived incredibly simple lives. They wore the same clothes over and over again. They kept their junk to a minimum so they could really run far and fast with the Lord.

Finally I decided to try it. I was going to build my capsule wardrobe, and I was genuinely thrilled about it. But here's what happens when someone who is obsessed with her trappings attempts to pare down what she has: I just kept adding. I spent all of January frantically trying to shop and add to my wardrobe. *Well, if I'm not buying anything else, I really need these pants! Oh, oh, oh—I couldn't do a capsule wardrobe without this shirt.* The whole thing was utterly pathetic, and I found myself months later with a stuffed closet and a tired and frustrated heart.

This is the same story for a lot of us, right? It doesn't matter whether it's clothes, furniture, gadgets, cars, or a daily latte habit. Our life is filled with little things we're convinced we need to survive.

I don't believe this necessarily comes down to selfishness. I think we've forgotten that we're wild. We don't remember that we have a Father to supply all our needs. We've misplaced the truth that He loves us more than the lilies, which He clothes in splendor (Matthew 6:28–29). His love and presence are no longer what spices our life and makes our world sweet. So we gather, we buy, we collect, we curate, we wish-list, and we make Pinterest boards. We add things to our life and to our rhythms in the belief that it will one day be enough. But what if all these things we amass for ourselves and the hope of a better life are actually the very things that drag us down? If the capsule wardrobe is all about trimming down our closets to the essentials, then we can learn a thing or two through trimming down life's "stuff"—and our anxieties about that stuff—by going back to the essentials God has for us. We'll never have enough things to start our "capsule life" as long as we don't go back to the root of the issue and reclaim our identity as wild women.

Wild women have enough today—right now—because they have Him. Wild women know that He will bring the next meal, because that's what He does. Wild women appreciate the habitat He's placed them in and the people He's placed there for them to grow with. Wild women appreciate natural beauty, and they don't find their identity in how their world is perceived. Wild women know that kindness and joy and freedom make them beautiful and make their faces light up. Wild women know that the aroma of Christ and the wind of the Holy Spirit flowing through their home make it sweeter than any candle they could find at Anthropologie.

Yes, we live in a world filled to the brim with trappings. But if we want to go back to the wild, we have to be willing to pack light.

We can go back. We can be reborn wild. That's what this book is all about.

Wherever you are, however mundane or broken or idyllic your life is—whatever path you find yourself on—the wild and free life is waiting for you. It's been purchased on the cross, and the kingdom of God is waiting, heaving, groaning—ready for you to take your place. And it's never too late to say yes. The story isn't over. It's just getting started.

This is no fairy tale where you're relegated to wait inside an ivory tower until the men let you out or Jesus comes back. If you find yourself bruised and battered because you've been fighting for your place, or if you need some revival because you've been sitting sweetly for too long on folded hands—the time is now.

Let's go back to the garden where we were created whole, good, wild, and free. Let's look back at the cross of Christ, where we find freedom and liberty and refreshment and calling. Let's remember that we're daughters. Let's take our place as ambassadors.

Let's talk to our Dad as if He's really listening and actually cares. Let's live like He meets all of our needs. Let's leave behind our lives of sighing and waiting and wondering what would happen if we really stepped into the lives He has for us.

PRAYER

Holy Spirit, be gentle and complete, and come remind us of who You made us to be. Father, take the eyes of our hearts and set them firmly on You as we seek to understand our identity and what direction we should be pointed in. Give us ears to hear what You call us, and silence the world that is yelling at us from all sides. Take us back to the garden. Take us back to the wild, Father.

HAYLEY'S RESPONSE

I'll be honest. When we started talking about "wild and free," my first thought was, *Well, not too wild.* Maybe that was your initial gut feeling too. As I've studied Scripture, though, I believe if we are not walking wildly in who God created us to be, we're missing out on a large portion of our charge as believers. We were made in the image of God; our original mom and dad inhabited the wildest, lushest, and safest garden. That should have been our home too. However, things don't always go as hoped, and we've needed a Rescuer to pull us out of our mess. That doesn't mean we should stop reaching for our Eden identity, though. If you knew your rightful inheritance was a beautiful and exotic garden, would you not walk like it? Well, your eternal inheritance is that amazing, and it's OK to have a little wild, excited swagger in your step.

We Have Become Caged by Our Limitations

I can pick a girl out of a crowd—any small group, coffee shop, or cashier line—who is living defensively. I can peg her so easily because *I* often am her. I happen to be the kind of girl who likes to get small when threatened, hoping to disappear completely. The last thing I want to do is make a fuss. I will try hard not to stand out. In fact, I'll wear a slew of tastefully put-together neutrals, hoping to simply blend into the crowd. Getting attention for *anything* will cause me discomfort. One of my deepest fears is being misunderstood, so I go out of my way to avoid any hint of controversy.

This is what it looks like to live defensively.

When we're little, we learn quickly to avoid the hot stove, hold our mama's hand, and not run into traffic. We're taught to look both ways and to say please and thank you. We are trained on how to handle life. And because pain is part of life, we learn to develop defense mechanisms.

When some animals get frightened, they get really small and ball up really tight. I think of one of those roly-poly bugs I used to catch when I was a little girl. They'd be skittering in and out of my grandma's pots of begonias, up and over the side into the moist soil, out and down to the concrete. One little tap, and they'd clench up as hard as a fist. Their protection was the hard exterior, keeping the soft stuff safe from the outside world.

Other animals, in response to fear, try to make themselves as large and loud as possible. This masks how they are really feeling—inferior, nervous, and threatened. They get really big to distract the world from seeing how very small they really are. Think of a puffer fish. When threatened, it puts on a show of crazy proportions, making sure its enemies know who is in charge.

Do you remember a moment in your life that made you want to tuck your legs up under you and disappear? Or did you get loud, making sure other people knew not to mess with you? What was it that made you feel like you had to protect yourself? Was it an overheard whisper or seeing something you couldn't unsee? Maybe it was the criticism of someone trusted and dear to you. Maybe it was a feeling you got from being at home alone as an only child or squished between a bunch of siblings. Maybe you embarrassed yourself in a way you thought was irredeemable.

We learn to live defensively at a really young age—and like in the animal kingdom, that fear often shows itself in different ways. Sadly, even the most protected and cherished little girls will still encounter the world beyond what their parents can control. Also, because of our sinful nature, the sin of others, and the fallen condition of the world, things that are not malicious at all can still wound us like a paper cut that won't heal.

Families break up. Bullies show up at recess. War and famine and heartbreak prowl the corners of the world and the channels on your TV. We mess up and make poor decisions. We fall short of expectations or we hurt the people we love. The world is an unpredictable place if nothing else.

So we learn to live defensively within this broken world. We begin to act in a way we believe protects us. Our environments and God-given personalities play into our defenses, and it's all tinged with the brokenness that cloaks the fallen earth. Some of us learn to not rock the boat and not step on toes. Others of us rail against expectations and rebel at every turn. Most of us at some point hold on to unforgiveness and shame, and we hide or deflect rather than endure an uncomfortable healing. This is the way of a woman who has grown to love the comfort afforded her by her own defense mechanisms. I know this firsthand.

It is only through a daily yielding to the safety I find in my Father's world that I am able to open up, unclench my fists, and lay down my defenses. The same is true of my friends who would rather get bigger and fight—they must yield their desire to get bigger than their fears. It is because we know we are seen and kept by our heavenly Father that we can put down our armor and unfurl our hearts.

The Many Camouflages of a Woman Living Defensively

We've all learned methods to protect ourselves. Not one of us is immune to the temptation to live defensively. We find ways to self-soothe and cope with what threatens us. I want to help you identify the ways you self-protect, but it's too simplistic to give you a check-list to figure out what your defense mechanism is. Instead, let's look at some other women's stories. You may see yourself reflected in how one (or several!) of these women protect themselves.

The Iron Woman

"People never believe me when I say I'm fine. But what do they expect me to say? Everyone has been hurt, and most people are tired. Life has to go on, and really, I'm OK. It's not that bad anyway. I thought I'd marry him, but it didn't work out, and that's life. It kind of frustrates me when people expect me to be upset about it, because things just don't always work out. Some might call it denial, but I prefer to see it as strength. My worst nightmare is running into someone from high school in the grocery store. They probably only heard the news on Facebook. The last thing I want is to see the pity in their eyes. I am really, really fine."

The Achiever

"I've worked really hard to get to where I am, and I don't think it's too much to expect to be respected for it. People should know who I am and not speak to me like they do sometimes. It really irritates me when people don't know who I am. I hate that sometimes people think I'm unimportant, especially people I respect."

The Scared and Small

"My biggest fear is getting shut down—told no, told I'm out of line, told I'm too much. So if I keep quiet and small in the first place, I figure this won't ever happen. I could be more fun or more vivacious, but that might bring criticism. After all, it's hard to put myself out there. I do *not* want a spotlight. And I do not want to bother anyone. I just want to sit on the sidelines, unnoticed and left alone. It's safer that way."

The Regretter

"I was a really good kid. I have a lot of sweet childhood memories. But a lot has changed since then. I've done things my mother would disown me for if she knew. Sometimes it feels like a secret that is beating in my heart, the memories of decisions I've made. I know I can't go back and change what I did, and I think that's the hardest part about it all. I feel like I'm stuck this way forever because I don't get a do-over."

The Controller

"My day planner is my most important possession—like, I'd grab it before photo albums if there was a fire. If I get off my schedule, it ruins my day, and don't get me started about other people being late. When things don't go how I've planned, or if I just don't know the plan someone else has made, I can feel my shoulders getting tense. I keep to-do lists of to-do lists, but it makes me feel steady. Nothing puts me more off-kilter than when things don't go my way."

The Challenger

"When I disagree with something, I'm not afraid to let you know. I feel like I'm always defending my position. It doesn't bother me; it feels important to make sure people know what I think. Sometimes it offends other people, but I feel like maybe they're being sensitive. It's like standing up for yourself . . . if you don't, who will?"

The Restless Wanderer

"I wonder sometimes if I'm running away when things get hard. I don't know if I've always been this way, but as I look back over the past several years, I'm not sure I can deny it. I changed my major a few times, making me a little late to graduate. When I get lonely in a city, I can tell it's time for me to move on. I always have a nagging feeling that there is something better just around the corner."

The Busy Bee

"I haven't been home at my house for longer than thirty minutes since last month. Somehow I always end up on the go. I have tons of friends, and it's always really fun to try to see them as much as possible. When I'm in my car, I have the music on. When I fall asleep, it's to reality television. I call my mom when I'm working out. One time, I had a friend ask me if it was hard for me to sit alone with my thoughts. I do know that silence really bothers me, and I don't like to sit still for too long."

The Victim

"I think sometimes that life is harder for me than it should be. I look at other people who have perfect families or great jobs, and I wonder why I didn't get to have that kind of life. I don't have tons of people who care about me. I don't love my job. I don't feel great about my body. I wonder if I have ever really been loved. When I get sad or scared, I spend a lot of my time thinking about or reading about what might be wrong with me. I don't know if any of it is even fixable, but I'd at least like to know why life is hard for me."

The Perfectionist

"If I'm going to do something, it's worth doing well. I don't just say yes—I go all out. My word is my honor. I have a hard time letting go sometimes because it feels like it could always be better. If something is less than perfect, I'm annoyed. The flaws haunt me, and I always vow to do better in the future."

////

Whether you're a perfectionist, the small and scared type, the victim, or some combination of the above, defense mechanisms are a poor substitute for wild and free living. Maybe you've played this part for so long that you've forgotten who you were really made to be. The truth is, it's awfully hard to remember the wild voice of your Father when you're so busy playing it safe.

Maybe you're the child of divorced parents, constantly taking on the impossible task of making both sides happy.

Maybe your classmates picked on you as a kid, and now you try to blend in as much as possible.

Maybe you are afraid of being forgotten, so you dress to kill and plead for love.

Maybe you're sitting with shame, and the only way to drown it is a Netflix binge, night after night.

Maybe you get mouthy and try to hard-sell others on your opinion before they realize you're the fraud you believe yourself to be.

Maybe you've learned to assess each situation you're in and proceed accordingly so you stay inside the lines and are able to please everyone around you.

Whether you feel like you're not enough or way too much, these defense mechanisms are completely of our own making. We live too often by the rules we've set for ourselves. We've gotten used to defaulting to our chosen defense. The rules we've set allow us to believe we're safe from feeling out of control or vulnerable again. We're curled up, with clenched fists. We've set our jaws, built our cages, and shut the world out.

And we all need to be freed.

Meekness May Not Mean
What You Think It Means

I remember distinctly the first time I felt like I was too much. I was about seven.

I am the typical oldest daughter in almost every way. I have two little brothers, and I was getting the sense that if I wasn't careful, I would outshine them. My parents started to tell me to tone it down, in not so many words.

It was well-intentioned parenting, but I have to check myself every day to make sure I'm not doing it with my boys. I don't want my children to feel they have to fit into a mold the size of my preferences.

I remember one day in particular when my family was enjoying a rare day off. Both of my parents worked full-time, so we lived for the weekends. The air was thick and hot, and I was excited to be spending time with my parents, especially my dad.

We packed up a bag of baseballs and a tiny bat and drove to the park in our little town. We chose a baseball diamond from the uninhabited many, and I squared up to the plate and kicked the dirt that was still wet from an early spring rain. A few feet away from me was my pitcher-father, who had abandoned the mound and made his way closer to me. He lobbed a ball in my direction, and I made contact with a sharp "clink." I was giddy. With pure joy, I jumped up and down, I glowed, and I looked to my mom and dad's faces for approval.

Yet as I prepared to take another turn, my dad shushed me, letting me know we were really there for my preschool brother to hit baseballs, and I needed to be in the outfield. This wasn't about taking turns—my dad wanted my brother to be athletic and not overshadowed by his big sister. But what I heard from my dad on that day still rings in my heart: *Hush; make yourself small; make room for others.* My dad meant no harm, but my heart that is bent toward untruth believed a lie.

I believed I should be small so I would be valued. I believed I should be small because quiet and small girls are the most loved. I believed living at my full capacity would make my brother feel insecure about his abilities. I shouldn't be too big or make my brother feel too small.

As a young woman, I believed I should be small so my Christian brothers could be elevated. I bought into the idea that for them to be respected, I needed to be less. In order for them to be pure, I had to be so lacking in allure that I'd hardly be noticeable at all. I felt any space I took up was harmful to someone else. I felt like a walking stumbling block.

There is a whole generation of women who are living this way—who have been told to live defensively, because we have massively misunderstood what it means to be meek.

Making room for others is not a bad thing by any means, but it turns on us when we allow that desire to become more about being liked and comfortable than about obeying the Lord. I'll be honest. Sometimes it feels really good to be small and scared. Many of us have learned to be comfortable curled up tight. But when we live that way, it's certainly not the kind of meek of which Scripture speaks.

Many of you are familiar with 1 Peter 3:3–4: "Your beauty should not come from outward adornment, such as elaborate hair-styles and the wearing of gold jewelry or fine clothes. Rather, it should be that of your inner self, the unfading beauty of a *gentle* and quiet spirit, which is of great worth in God's sight" (emphasis mine). Many have used this verse to underscore the idea that the godly woman is a quiet woman, a woman who doesn't take up space and doesn't speak out of turn. But this use of *gentle* (or *meek*) does not mean being a pushover or hidden from sight. Sure, it means we should not speak in a way that needlessly stirs up friction or destructive commotion. But a closer look at this word in its original language reveals a new dimension.

The Greek word *praus* is used in 1 Peter 3:4 to describe the characteristic of gentleness or meekness. HELPS Word-studies define this word as "exercising *God's strength* under *His control*—i.e. demonstrating power without undue harshness."[6] The heart of meekness is simply harnessing the Lord's power under His control.

This Greek word is also used in Matthew 5:5, giving the meaning of *meek* a new spin: "Blessed are the *meek*, for they will inherit the earth" (emphasis mine). Do you see? Biblical meekness is never weakness. Rather, it is a harnessing of God-given strength.

When I made room for my brother as a small girl, it was because I wanted to please and fit in. But now when I make room for him, it's because I love him. That's not weakness—it's harnessed strength.

What Holds Women Back from Free Living

God has created women as incredibly varied and individual beings. There are so many beautiful facets to a woman—I see this in the lives of the women I do everyday life with. But I also believe something is holding us back.

Here is one thing I believe to be true of most women: We are living defensively rather than living wildly and freely. We are bound up by our own fears and self-imposed limitations rather than walking freely in God's purpose for our lives.

The defensive posture plays out differently for all of us.

In a world that calls out, "Do big things!" and "You can have it all!" it's easy to feel like we're not enough. And when this happens, sometimes our defense is to become large and in charge, convincing everyone we really can do it.

On the other hand, when we feel like we're way too much, our defense can be to make ourselves small and fade into the corner. Suddenly we wish we could simply erase ourselves on the spot, along with whatever "too much" thing we just did or said.

Here's the thing. Feeling too much, feeling not enough—these are two sides of the same coin. They both limit us as women created to live wild and free. You may lean more toward one or the other, or you may feel like you experience both all at once.

Wherever you are, God is calling you to freedom.

But before we can truly walk in His freedom, we need to understand what holds us back. I see women living defensively in response to four pressure points common to all of us.

The Expectations of Others

What are the expectations in your family of origin? Your place of origin? Were you brought up in a hardworking Midwestern town where you bundled up and waved to the neighbors from the safety of your SUV? Were you taught that it was best to mind your own business and let people be? Maybe you, like me, were the oldest daughter, and you decided to pipe down so you wouldn't make too much of a fuss.

Maybe you're like my good friend who was told to be successful—that only the very best of the best are valuable. Maybe you come from the kind of family where holiness is the family business. You had to toe the line and look the part, even if you were struggling with your faith. Maybe beauty and physical perfection were expectations in your family, and you teetered there, always trying to stay just thin and lovely enough.

What are the expectations you find yourself faced with now? Does it feel like the people in your community, your place of employment, or your church have a tacit understanding of how women are to behave? Are you trying to fit in and make yourself "just so"? Most of the time, there are no actual rules for behavior spelled out, but the culture can tell a different tale.

I've been a part of groups of women where it was expected that you'd stay at home and homeschool your kids. I've run around with people with whom it was the norm to climb every social and career ladder you could find. I've been a part of supercreative groups of women where you were expected to put your talents to work. I've felt like way too much in some situations and completely not enough in others. The truth is, it's never an individual who sets the tone for the group. Rather, it's an amalgam of everyone's experiences and expectations. However, the tone set in any group of people can give us a set of expectations to live up to.

When I was little, my family's rule was that you couldn't make a fuss about what you ordered at a restaurant. You always had to be agreeable and very easy on the waiter. You ordered it exactly as stated on the menu, and you took whatever you got, even if the restaurant goofed up. My dad still pokes fun at a few of my friends when he remembers how picky they were when we'd go through a drive-through.

Now, this expectation itself isn't harmful or wrong. But when you add in that I was a compliant, people-pleasing child, I eventually felt I shouldn't speak up about my real tastes. As I carried that mentality into my adulthood, it wasn't driven by a desire to love someone else well; I became chained to the expectations of my family of origin.

It's taken some time, but I've learned to throw out that expectation and order what I want. I'm not obnoxious, but if I want extra pickles, I'll certainly ask. I figure if I'm paying for my food, I may as well order what I really want!

But we don't necessarily need to buck all expectations. As you consider the expectations you live by, use discernment. Some are destructive, and some are for your benefit. The woman who reacts to feeling not enough by puffing herself up, for example, may be tempted to defy all expectations, whether or not those expectations are for her good. If her cultural norms demand she go to college immediately after high school, she may abandon that path altogether. If it's expected that she'll get a high-powered job, she may catch the first flight to Africa to serve without a paycheck. Or a woman who feels the pressure to conform to a particular beauty standard may throw off all cares about external aesthetics.

There's no need to abide by social conventions or expectations that don't serve you or others well. This idea of being small and not making a fuss doesn't serve real-life, grown-up women. You can take up all the space you need and still leave room for others. You can be seen *and* heard and still be gracious. Challenging expectations is wise, but abandoning them defensively is not. Romans 12:2 reads, "Don't copy the behavior and customs of this world, but let God transform you into a new person by changing the way you think. Then you will learn to know God's will for you, which is good and pleasing and perfect" (NLT). You can push back on the ways culture bosses you around and still listen to those who love you well.

The Quest for Control

When I was thirteen, an awkward stage for just about any girl, my parents' marriage suffered irreconcilable differences. As my dad told me the news from across the table of a Ruby Tuesday restaurant, I felt the world falling away around me. The ground I trusted and the bedrock I rested on quietly crumbled as he explained the ins and outs of what would become our new normal. In that moment, I felt like I was left to lead myself. From that point on, I lost trust in anyone else to take care of me.

I saw that my parents were embroiled in their own strife. I was old enough to see some of the reality of the situation, but I didn't yet have the societal and psychological construct to understand the nuances. I just believed that I'd better learn to take care of myself, because my parents were busy looking after their own problems.

It is the very nature of this fallen earth to let us down and leave us fractured. This is the cultural brokenness you and I have grown up in. Maybe your family was intact, but you suffered through years of church abuse, leaving you unsure of how to navigate authority. Maybe you've had toxic friendships that have crippled your ability to make real and healthy connections. Whatever this brokenness has looked like in your life, it's worth taking time to note some of the ways you've experienced the fallout.

I believe this brokenness has imprinted in our very nature the need to regain control. We might have lost it once, but we'll never make that mistake again, we tell ourselves. So we start to take the stance of, "I can take care of myself, thank you very much." We'd rather cut our losses and preemptively put up barriers to make sure we never get hurt again than trust that others really do want what is best for us. After all, we've heard it before.

We carefully manage our words, our actions, and our images to steer clear of vulnerability. We answer, "I'm fine," whether or not it's the truth.

Have you ever seen someone come completely undone? You know what I mean—the ugly cry. The mascara-turned-mess. The unfiltered, let-it-all-out moment of grief. That's exactly what we're afraid of. This fear of coming undone—that's why we stay neat and tidy and *always* in control. We're afraid of showing too much emotion and being labeled "hysterical." We worry what people will think if we don't have it all together.

A creative young woman I know who grew up with a single mother said, "I have figured out in my life that I've never had a leader I could trust or one who has led me well. Therefore, I've felt like I've had to take control of my own circumstances. Meanwhile, God is patiently waiting for me to trust Him as my leader and believe that He has my best interests in mind. He is trustworthy. The opposite of faith isn't doubt; it's control."

I believe she's on to something. If we dedicate ourselves to meticulous life management that doesn't lean on faith in a good God, we are signing ourselves up for a life of anxiety that comes from constantly chasing control. What if we chose a better way? Jesus makes this promise to us: "Peace I leave with you; my peace I give you. I do not give to you as the world gives. Do not let your hearts be troubled and do not be afraid" (John 14:27).

The Fear of Failure

If you're not living in freedom, you're living in fear. Fear and love cannot occupy the same space, and neither can deep-rooted fear and freedom. Everyone starts to look like an enemy who could hurt you. You stop being able to see people for their God-given worth but start seeing them as people who might sideline your hopes for life.

I am really afraid of conflict. I don't just shy away from it—it full-on terrifies me. That fear plays a large part in my life. My friendship with Jess has been hugely helpful in growing and healing in this area of fear (because she's the fearless type!), but it's something I continue to work on.

Let me tell you how this plays out in my real life. I never, ever listen to my voice mails, because what if someone who calls is mad at me? I dread looking at my emails, because what if someone who emailed is disappointed in me? I get nervous when someone asks to get coffee or says they "need to talk," because what if I've let them down?

As you can see, this is a deep-rooted problem in my life.

If I could armchair-diagnose myself, I would say this fear comes from the fact that my family growing up never directly dealt with our wounds. We just let the relationship grow cold until enough time had passed that we could all act like we forgot it ever happened. Any time there was conflict in my family, there was a break in relationship and a loss of intimacy.

I have to speak truth to myself all the time, and having close relationships is sometimes really hard for me. I have a tendency to just let friends go once I've disappointed them or hurt them. I feel like we'll both be better off that way.

This is not something I can preach at you from a position of victory and healing. This is a real-time, true-life example of unbelief and struggle in my life. I teeter between fearing what people think of me, wanting to appear good to them, and despairing over perceived loss of relationship. None of these things line up with the gospel of grace and forgiveness.

Fear has ruled my life and rung in my ears. It is a dance that has made me crazy for years, and sometimes I still can't quite shake it. Sometimes I still have obsessive thoughts about this fear of conflict, and I still sinfully respond in selfish self-protection.

Your bouts with fear may look different than mine, but I suspect you know what it's like to go to battle with something so frightening that your cheeks get hot just thinking about it. Maybe that pit-in-your-stomach feeling has lingered for years.

But God lovingly calls us to cast our cares on Him (1 Peter 5:7). It's a work in progress, to be sure. Will you work through it with me? He is our refuge. He will lift us out of our debilitating fear. And guess what? He's already found us out—our worst fears and failures and all—and He's chosen us anyway. So we can believe Him when He says He'll protect us and keep us.

The Shame Cycle

If you're living in unforgiveness or shame, it will steal every bit of freedom you have. You can't move forward if you're tethered to the ugly pain of the past.

Whether you're the one who needs forgiving or you're holding back your forgiveness from someone else, you need to bring that junk into the light. If you need forgiveness from someone, go and ask them. Bring yourself low and step into the light, knowing that Jesus is right there with you. Confess your yuck and ask forgiveness for the sin you committed and for the pain you caused. There is nothing like the freedom that comes from confession and repentance.

First John 4:7–19 is a rich passage of Scripture that beautifully reveals how God is love:

> Dear friends, let us love one another, for love comes from God. Everyone who loves has been born of God and knows God. Whoever does not love does not know God, because God is love. This is how God showed his love among us: He sent his one and only Son into the world that we might live through him. This is love: not that we loved God, but that he loved us and sent his Son as an atoning sacrifice for our sins. Dear friends, since God so loved us, we also ought to love one another. No one has ever seen God; but if we love one another, God lives in us and his love is made complete in us. This is how we know that we live in him and he in us: He has given us of his Spirit. And we have seen and testify that

the Father has sent his Son to be the Savior of the world. If anyone acknowledges that Jesus is the Son of God, God lives in them and they in God. And so we know and rely on the love God has for us. God is love. Whoever lives in love lives in God, and God in them. This is how love is made complete among us so that we will have confidence on the day of judgment: In this world we are like Jesus. There is no fear in love. But perfect love drives out fear, because fear has to do with punishment. The one who fears is not made perfect in love. We love because he first loved us.

What do you think? Doesn't this sound better than the alternative of staying stuck in unforgiveness? The fact that God has forgiven us and thrown off our shame is our launching point for offering forgiveness to others. Together, we can come into the light and know the kind of love that only God is.

Shame has no place in love. Fear has no place in love. Unforgiveness has no place in love. These things are not of the Lord.

Conviction brought by the Holy Spirit is not to be confused with shame. Holy conviction leads to repentance, while shame only leads to bondage and hiding. Shame cannot exist in the light, though it flourishes in the darkness.

However, it can be just as destructive to withhold forgiveness from someone who needs it. We have been forgiven much, and it doesn't reflect the gospel or God's abundant mercy to hold back forgiveness from someone else.

I recently experienced a startling and burning conviction about a relationship I'd let wither because of my own refusal to forgive. Instead of being brave and facing the conflict, I avoided confrontation and allowed the friendship to fall away. The problem was that we still saw each other all the time, and as the months passed, my heart was getting harder toward her. I thought I had chosen the easier path by glossing over the problem, but in reality, I had made it so much harder—and more awkward—for both of us.

Because I so viscerally dislike conflict, I tested the waters with a text to this friend. I clocked twelve sweaty minutes waiting for her reply, but once she replied that she'd been in the same boat, I immediately felt relief that I had shoved this situation into the light. Now we get to experience the gospel goodness of forgiveness; we get to be in fellowship with our Father and with each other; and we're both braver for the next time hurt or shame arises.

If you are one who doesn't hide from a conflict, it may be tempting to criticize first, lest you be criticized. It's much easier to cast shame on others than admit we've been wrong.

Responding to shame and a lack of forgiveness can lead us to behave that way. However, holding conflict with open hands and trusting the Lord to convict the other person can be freeing for you. If you are dealing with another believer, you can trust that God is working in their life too. You may not trust the person, but you can trust God.

Ultimately, we have all been forgiven so much. We have no right to withhold forgiveness from ourselves or others. Seek God for forgiveness for your own faults and then throw off the shame because God has forgiven you. You need only ask. If you need to forgive someone else, it will bring you so much lightness of spirit to just do so.

Freedom from Defensive Living

As women of freedom, we're not called to live defensively, whether by playing dead or putting on a show. We're invited to live boldly in the light, calling others to join us. If we know the Father, we should be drawn more and more to the light as we get to know

Him better. The light feels revealing, but it also feels good because Jesus is in the light. In Him there is no darkness, and He does not dwell in the darkness. When we are brave and expose our own sin, we walk out of darkness into the light, where repentance and holy acceptance can occur.

We can experiment with leaving defensive living behind. We can rock the boat; we can let go of control; we can break the mold and not meet expectations. We can risk stepping on toes without the fear of losing a relationship. We can do all this because we don't have to fear losing our relationship or standing with God. We believe in His power to reconcile.

PRAYER

Father, the gospel is about nothing if it is not about wildly trusting that You are bigger than our comfort, our desires, and our fears. The good news is that we are reconciled to You through the death and resurrection of your Son, Jesus, wholly loved by You our Father and invited as Your daughters to take part in eternal life.

We all live small and scared sometimes. When we are wounded, we rightly believe that the world is not a safe place. But, God, You are a safe place. You are our refuge and our hiding place. We are found whole in You.

Let us throw off our earthly responses to feeling "less than." Let us stop playing dead and stop putting on a show. Let us live wholly and rightly with You, trusting that You see us and know us and have accepted us all the same. Praise You for Your Holy Spirit, who comforts us and shifts our hearts closer to You.

Lord, forgive us for the ways we've offended You in our defense mechanisms. Forgive us for the ways we've bought into the world's lies of how we should react and live. Let us look first to You in how to respond. Let us trust You to care for us. Let us trust You to champion our cause. We love You, Lord. Amen.

JESS'S RESPONSE

For the record, I love seeing women come undone. As a pastor's wife, a friend, and a leader, I find that nothing bums me out more than when I see the tears well up and the voice get shaky and then the gal I'm talking to stuffs it back down. Whatever she wanted to say, whatever was burning in her heart—I want to hear it. I feel safe to be my own broken and twisted self when she lets what's really in her heart come out. I dare you, ladies. Let it come undone. Don't apologize for your tears or qualify how you feel. God isn't freaked out by our pain or what we're really feeling; He just wants us to share it with Him rather than bury it and pretend like it's not there. He is here to listen and here to love.

God of the Wild

I left the dorms my freshman year of college determined to come back a new woman. The past year had been my first real attempt at finding my place in Christian community, and it had also been my first real failure. For me, college was the beginning of being faced with a lot of my inadequacies in a larger Christian community. There was always someone prettier, kinder, neater, smarter—and there were plenty of girls who served more. The enemy and I took turns speaking untruths over me as I told myself when I left for the summer, *I will not come back a mess. I will not come back as the funny, fat friend. I will not come back needy. I will get my junk together and be better.*

A few weeks later, I rejoined my college friends at a massive worship event, the Passion Conference, which was designed for tens of thousands of college students to call on the name of the Lord together. For me, the major pitfall was that the event was held outdoors as a camping event, and there is almost nothing I abhor more than being outside for an extended period of time. Since I genuinely was so expectant to worship the Lord with my friends *and* it would have made me lame to admit I hate camping, I signed up and pretended I was totally jazzed about it.

I think I'm finally at the place where I can giggle about all that went wrong in those few days, now that I'm twelve years out from that horrific experience, but I still refuse to go camping again— ever. It started with the food poisoning I got from a bad hamburger the night before the trip started. I spent the fifteen-hour van ride with friends, moaning in pain and sprinting to the pavement to get sick once we'd stopped for gas. Just as we were arriving at the ranch where the event was held, I realized my stomach pains had turned into period cramps, and yeah . . . that was coming. Our first night of camping, a torrential rainstorm flooded our tents with a few inches of water, promptly ruining all our clothing and the beloved products I desperately needed for my period. I got chigger bites from sitting on the ground (which I always knew was a bad idea), and if you don't know what a chigger is—don't Google it. Spare yourself, and I'll tell you it's a disastrous little bug that forms a small hole in human skin, chews on your flesh, and leaves you itching like a madwoman.

We'd arrived at the campsite a few days early. The night before the main worship event, I sat by myself about a mile away from our tent, looking out over the land, genuinely trying to have a moment with the Lord. What better time for a second superabundant rainstorm to blow through, leaving me soaked and lost inside the thick walls of rain. I couldn't move forward. I couldn't move backward. I just sat and talked to the Lord. I told him I didn't understand why He was crushing my idyllic day of worship—or, rather, I was crushing it with my own awkward, clumsy, things-go-wrong ways. I just wanted to have a sweet day with my hands in the air and the breeze blowing gently. I wanted to feel the warm fuzzies of being close and intimate with Him. I wanted an experience that was good for me, that would make me become wiser and feel more at peace with who He made me to be.

The next morning, I stood on a field with tens of thousands of other college students eager to be with God. All of my ailments were reaching a fever pitch: sensitive stomach, itchy legs, menstruation and cramps galore, plus the breeze was not even slightly blowing, and the Texas sun was giving me second-degree sunburns on my shoulders. My friends and I were sitting adequately close to the stage (which everyone knows usually has a direct correlation to how close you are to God), but at an awkward angle so we couldn't see the words on the screen and thus were unable to sing along to most of the songs—all of which were new to us. In spite of all that, I learned what worship truly was that day.

The tame and scripted worship of God that gave me warm and fuzzy feelings never came that day, and at the same time, my mental picture of God's glory was blown to bits. Up until then, worship had been about how I felt; on that day, God expanded my viewpoint to see that He is not wildly concerned with how I feel but is wildly out for His own glory. Singing to Him, praying to Him, talking about Him, learning more about His nature and goodness and work in our lives—this all benefits us, but it's not *about* us. The point of our worship is not our joy or our advancement. God's sole purpose in calling His people to worship Him is allowing them to give Him glory because He wants it.

God's laser focus on His glory, above all else, speaks of wild abandon to me. It's the same kind of unrestrained adoration I wish I had toward Him and His kingdom and His cause as well. You know when you meet a woman on a mission, one who won't be detoured or dismantled? You can see the spark in her eye, and it stirs up something in you—you could almost just sit and watch her, whether she's cooking up a fantastic meal or building a nonprofit. When I start to really look and see how God reigns over His creation, constructing beings for the exclusive purpose of allowing them to magnify His greatness—*that* is wild to me. And I want to watch Him, see Him more clearly, and take it all in.

When I reflect on the character of God, I see so many attributes that make Him truly worthy of worship. But the fact that He is and always has been about one thing and one thing chiefly—His own glory—is always the most surprising. I'm the kind of gal who needs to know my purpose and have it defined really clearly before

I enter into something. And yet, I'll be completely honest and tell you that when I began my relationship with the Lord and started walking with Him, I thought it was about me. I was convinced it was for me to feel better, for me to get more out of life, for me to go to heaven, and for me to just become an all-around better person. But our actions, our feelings, our lives do not keep the earth spinning.

And this is good news, right? We are not the main character in the greatest story ever told. This takes the pressure off. We can all breathe easy now. In the same way that we feel truly alive when we see a vast night sky or a huge, expansive ocean, the greatness and bigness of God free us up for wild worship instead of small living.

Our Father created us for His glory and created our world for His glory. He chose His people for His glory; He rescues us for His glory; and He raises up leaders among us for His glory. He defeats our enemies for His glory; He gives us victory for His glory; He draws us near after we sin for His glory; and He saves us for His glory.

Jesus was about His Father's glory. Jesus called us to good works for the glory of God; He suffered for God's glory; and He made a way for us on the cross so we could be coheirs with Christ—for God's glory. The author of Hebrews writes, "The Son is the radiance of God's glory and the exact representation of his being, sustaining all things by his powerful word. After he had provided purification for sins, he sat down at the right hand of the Majesty in heaven" (Hebrews 1:3).

The residuals for us are incredible—there's no doubt. We get eternity, everlasting life, earthly spiritual abundance, and we get our needs met. We get the Holy Spirit; we get to be ambassadors for our glorious God—and so much more. But the surplus blessings that we inherit out of His love don't change the everlasting purpose of God's interactions with man—*He wants His glory*. And now that we've said it approximately thirty times in this chapter so far, what does that word *glory* even mean? The Hebrew word used most often in the Old Testament to describe what we're talking about here is *kabod*, which means "glorious, honor, abundance, splendor, dignity, reputation, reverence."

If God's glory is His ultimate purpose, this shifts everything about how we view Him. When we stumble into the easy mistake of thinking that God is about us or His purpose is solely to do our will and our bidding, it makes Him so small. It may seem comforting for a second that the God of the universe has given us His full attention and is at our command, until we realize we've made Him very small in serving us. But, sweet sister friends, our God is so incredibly big. He is perfectly infinite. And it is this very fullness and completeness that He offers us in our anxieties when we feel we are too much and not enough. He is more in control than we could ever perceive, and He is wildly in love with you and concerned with the details of your life. You are never too much for Him! And you are always just enough to the God who lovingly created you.

As we're thinking about glory and trying to understand the concept, we don't have to look too far into our own worlds. Let's take a moment to look at people in our culture who get glory. Politicians, celebrities, Christian pastors and leaders, and—my personal favorite, of course—reality TV stars. We ascribe some sort of reverence to them, varying with how well-known they are and how potentially successful they are. We like to see into their daily lives through social media or pictures that the paparazzi can get, but for the most part, we realize they are incredibly set apart.

They ride in luxury jets far up in the sky. They live in large houses behind gated walls, with security guards keeping watch for anyone who would get too close. The income gap isn't the only thing that separates us—they just seem special and somewhat untouchable, am I right? We might, in a moment of boldness, ask for an autograph or ask for prayer, but we wouldn't see them and immediately cuddle with them or share their can of soda. We'd probably get arrested if we tried that.

But here is what makes our God so wild. He is *good* beyond our mind's comprehension. He cannot fail, not in anything He tries and not in loving any one of His creations. By His very nature, He cannot be imperfect. He is also *holy*, which means He is set apart—unlike anything else in the universe, He is worthy of complete devotion as one perfect in goodness and righteousness. He is all-powerful, all-knowing, infinite, sovereign, and incredibly faithful. Essentially when we set aside our human celebrities and leaders, we consecrate them, but this God—He is the only one truly worthy of being set aside and honored and put on a pedestal to worship.

The phrase "fear of the Lord" is a trip wire for so many women (and men) because it's hard to reconcile a God who is to be feared and who can also draw us close. We are comfortable with reverence. We know how it feels to put someone or something on a pedestal and adore them, because we do it with our leaders, our celebrities, and our stars. The difference between the Lord and the humans we undeservingly revere is how the subject of our worship responds. When we direct our praise toward humans, they rarely draw us closer. Celebrities don't invite us over for coffee after we follow them on Instagram, and famous pastors don't call to pray for us.

Our holy fear and reverence of the Lord is wildly different, though. It ends in our gain, our intimacy with Him, and our identity being built up and solidified. Setting God higher than ourselves doesn't mean He is untouchable. Proverbs 1:7 tells us that the fear of the Lord is the beginning of wisdom. The act of acknowledging, "You're up there. You're bigger. You're totally perfect. You're totally good. You can do whatever you want. You're worthy of my worship, and ultimately, I cannot control You," is the first step in knowing God better and genuinely walking with Him.

Worldly fear drives us away from the objects of our reverence, but the fear of the Lord pulls us in closer. Our God, in His wildness, has flipped fear on its head and made it as holy as He is. Where we could have been called subjects, He has called us daughters. Where He could continue to separate Himself, He has continued to draw close. Psalm 25:14 tells us that the friendship of the Lord is for those who fear Him, and He makes known to them His covenant.

Our God is wild in His very nature because He is all about His glory, for good reason. He is wild because He is consecrated and set apart and worthy of our absolute adoration and praise. But what makes Him most wild is that these things do not separate us from His love or protection. Rather, when we walk in knowledge and worshipful affirmation of His holiness, we get close to Him. That hard day I spent trying to muster up happy feelings while worshiping and camping was not my most intimate-feeling experience with the Lord. But something shifted in my heart and in my walk with Him that opened up my spirit to a truer version of worship. Just like we're able to love our friends better when we know them more confidently, our devotion and praise get that much sweeter when we see our Father in His true state—good, wild, big, and worthy.

The Relentless Love of a Wild God

God's ultimate priority of His glory would be wild enough all on its own. The beautiful and reverent fear plus the intimacy that permeates our relationship with Him—that's remarkable. And yet, another facet to the wild truth about who our God is will, if we let it, absolutely blow our minds and leave us in astounded praise. Our Father isn't just holy beyond all other things and worthy of our holy fear; He is also wildly loving toward us. His love defies all reason, all common sense, and any condition of reward or return. It's just that crazy.

Thankfully, the love of God can carry the weight of a thousand metaphors. Throughout the Bible, it's almost as if He gives us layer after layer to unpeel, story after story to show us His love and devotion toward us—to help make this unfathomable, wild love just a little more fathomable to us. And listen, I'm thankful because I love a good metaphor, such as the one that describes our relationship with God as adoption into His family. Yet this imagery can often fall short for us because God didn't *just* adopt us. He didn't just let us into His family so we'd have somewhere to go, hoping we'd be a good addition. Our Father looked at us, while we were still sinners—even though He could foresee the full weight of how much we'd sin—and He paid the price to allow us into His family.

But it didn't stop there. Not only did He adopt us; He also made us co-heirs with His perfect Son, Jesus. He made us ambassadors—representatives—of his kingdom and His cause. He handed us the keys to the kingdom. He gave us the Holy Spirit to equip and empower us, and all the gifts we need to further His kingdom and live abundant lives.

If you've been around the church or Christian community for a while, you may have heard a bit about the book of Hosea. Hosea was an Old Testament prophet, a man with an incredibly hard job. Not only was he called to speak arduous truths, but the Lord also called him to live out the message he was preaching in personally painful ways.

The metaphor he was sharing with the world? Hosea was chosen to share that Israel—God's anointed people—was like an adulterous woman. God was setting Himself up as the relentlessly loving husband who would continually take her back, protect her, lavish grace on her, and do it all over again once she inevitably took off again. But Hosea's special assignment didn't end by just getting on a soapbox and telling everyone how broken they were. God called him to live a metaphorical story and *show* the lavish love and grace that only God could enable someone to have: "The LORD said to me, "Go, show your love to your wife again, though she is loved by another man and is an adulteress. Love her as the LORD loves the Israelites, though they turn to other gods and love the sacred raisin cakes" (Hosea 3:1).

That was essentially God's assignment: "Hosea, marry an adulterous woman. Pick one you're fairly certain will not be faithful, and then love her all the way to the end. She's going to have some children, and you're going to be pretty certain that one of them is not fathered by you. When she continuously leaves you—for things that are broken and don't fulfill her—go back and get her.

"That wife you love will become so lost that she'll wind up a slave, and at that point I want you to sell whatever you need to so you can get her back in your home. And speak kindly to her. And love her gently. And show her how she was wrong. And eventually, after lots of years and pain, you'll live as a devoted married couple. Those children, even the ones whose paternity you question— they'll be your children."

Do you see this? God is so wild that He transcends our expectations completely. This has to be one of the craziest stories in Scripture. And yet God is at the center of it, showing us His love in expectation-shattering ways.

If you've read Hosea or read any Christian fiction book depicting the story of Hosea and Gomer (goodness gracious, there are some good ones out there), you know that the story is heartrending and ultimately fairly easy to remove ourselves from if we want to. With emotional and physical affairs on the rise, even inside the church, this is a potential part of some of our stories. But for those of us who aren't married or haven't sinned in that particular way, let's not count our hearts out of needing this kind of saving.

I love how Hosea 3:1 says that the Lord loves His people, Israel, and will restore her, even though she abandons Him for raisin cakes. It's not always full-blown, massive affairs that take our hearts away from Him, is it? We love so many things more than we love our holy and fearful God. We love sports, our stuff, our churches, and our rules. We love our friends, our kids, and our reputations. We love creativity, our homes, and our opinions more than we love God. Ladies, I'll give it to you straight. Some days I feel like the candles in my house get more praise and devotion and thankfulness than my God gets.

Our hearts before we met Jesus were wandering around this earth, looking for something to put our hope and devotion into. Our hearts after meeting Jesus are still so prone to wander that we would leave Him for a raisin cake most days. But our Father—He knows this. So He made a way. He came after us with His relentless love.

It is not sensible or worldly wise, but God's love is wild. Rarely would any of us suggest to our sons or brothers or friends that they pick the most potentially unfaithful and prideful bride of the pack, but that is absolutely what our Father did when He chose us. Our love is often safe and guarded and motivated by reward. His love is fierce and without restraint, and we absolutely never deserve it or have the ability to earn it.

It doesn't stop with Hosea and Gomer either. God's Word is full of truth about His relentless love for us. Romans 8:39 tells us that *nothing* can separate us from God's love. Romans 5:8 reminds us that God's love was lavished on us while we were still sinners, before we worshiped or acknowledged Him. In Zephaniah 3, we're reminded that God quiets us with His love and that He sings over us loudly, rejoicing over His creation. First John 4:8 sums it up with the very strong and final word: Our God *is* love.

What's even crazier is, I don't think God stopped with biblical metaphors. I think He is still writing the definition of wild love all over each of our lives. When we can stop striving, running the calculations, and speculating over how to be the best Christian women we can possibly be, I think we'll see what's really going on.

We're all just adulterous women. Leaving our Father for raisin cakes—or salted caramel cake pops, am I right?—almost every chance we get. And He is extravagantly and seemingly foolishly extending grace over and over again, calling us back, picking us up, putting us back at the table with Him, and reminding us of who we are. Not for our comfort, but for His glory. For His very good pleasure. Because of His wild love.

God Is Bigger Than the Box We Put Him In

Here's the thing. If our God is so wild, we need to start acting a little wild ourselves. After all, like the very first wild woman, we are created in His image. If He is wild about his glory and relentless in His love, we are called to live likewise—as women made in His own image. And sometimes that means we need to let go of our tightly organized systems and plans.

I don't know about you, but I *love* my tightly organized systems and plans. All through my kids' toddler years, I'd plan out not just their meals but also their snacks days or weeks in advance. These days, I meticulously plan and schedule my social media posts. I keep around three running calendars and two master to-do lists. I have rhythms for when I meet with certain friends, do laundry, and read, and certain days of the week when I wash my hair. So when I bring this mind-set to church and apply it to my faith, then as you might guess, I run into a bit of trouble.

I can't deny it, and I won't hide it—I'm a church girl through and through. Something switched in me during my college years, and I felt this tug to the big local Baptist church, potentially the least sexy and exciting path a freshman in college could choose. I love the history of the church, even in all of her mistakes. I see swirls of freedom and passion inside of her, where I feel like a lot of others see containment and restriction.

It's no surprise, then, that the church is still my number one passion outside of my personal walk with Jesus and my family. My husband is a church planter of a sweet baby church that is currently coming out of the infancy stage and into the wide world of toddlerhood. We had our first service as Gospel Community in January 2014, and as of this writing, we've got about seventy people and are having the time of our lives. My husband loves to joke that we're "baptipresbycostal," but on paper we're officially nondenominational, and I don't care what kind of church you're used to, you'd be welcome at GC.

Can you picture our church? My friends Megan and Jeff sit on the front row with their hands sweetly raised. Lee stands in the back, holding and swaying baby Margot, while his wife, Julie, gets a break so she can sit and listen to the sermon. Davy is the most creative college student I've ever met. He sits on the left side, usually with two or three visitors—because he always brings visitors.

We've got people who take copious notes and probably know a lot more about the Bible than I do. We've got a few people hanging out in the back, dancing and using prayer language. Some of our friends are experts on all the church traditions, like baptism and communion, and some friends are just glad we have wine every few Sundays—even though they might not be sure why.

I love our church. Because I love these people.

But when we started the planting process, I found a pit of pride and hardness sitting in my heart that shocked and genuinely grossed me out. I consider myself a wild and free gal, and the idea for this book was well past the conception stage when the church was planted. Yet I found myself living with a very small and constricted notion of what women in the church should look like. It went way past the basic debates I see women living in—whether they should serve in the church, whether they should work or stay home with their families, and so forth. I'd settled in my heart that it was really healthy for believers to have varying viewpoints on those issues. And yet I still find some leftover expectations of women in my heart.

I expected women to grow and approach the Lord in the same ways I was used to. I expected they'd all pretty much want to wake up early to read the Bible, because that's what I liked to do. I expected they'd find comfort in being vulnerable and open with one another, because that's what was really good for me. Essentially, I anticipated they'd have vast opinions on a lot of things—but not on how to have a relationship with the Lord or what that should look like.

Those first few months of church planting were pretty laborious for me as I lived out my personal constraints. I was lonely. I waited patiently for my pastor-husband to set up some sort of system by which we could begin to indoctrinate all these other beautiful, wild women into *the way things were done.* I asked him about once a week, "When can we start discipleship or small groups?" I'd read all the books, and I knew that group growth could also happen organically, but I felt this fervent push in my heart to sit these gals down and hammer out a system of how we intended to advance together and really dig in.

During the past year, my husband has been patiently teaching me what it means to love a church, to love a people, outside of a super-established system, and I am so incredibly grateful. Our baby church would have collapsed and had the life squeezed out of it if we had made it as routine and rhythmic as the rest of my life. Inside the free-flowing community, I have found grace and life and, ultimately, women who love Jesus more than they love a system.

The first time I really talked to Sarah, I'm pretty sure we both cried. She's a college-age gal who just started coming to Gospel Community, and she is a massive blessing in my life. The night we met, we were in a small organic group that had gathered at my house to talk and pray through our dreams and goals. As she talked about her life, it seemed so eerily similar to mine—the trajectory she'd been on, the way the Lord had rescued her, and even our giftings seemed so similar. But something was drastically different about Sarah. She was wild and free in a way I could not really relate to, but I knew I had to put my finger on what it was. I viewed scheduled social media posts as ministry for the Lord (and they are!), but she talked about being up late the night before, leading a homeless woman to Jesus. The first time we talked about the Holy Spirit, the nuances of her language weren't lost on me. She didn't call Him "The Holy Spirit." She just called Him Holy Spirit, like you'd call your best friend Gina instead of "The Gina."

When I look at Sarah, I still see someone who is more like me than anyone else I think I've ever encountered, but I also see a woman who sees and knows that her God is wild. I genuinely believe she is not more comfortable in boxes, systems, or conformity because she knows that's not His character or His confinement, so why should it be hers?

What I learn from Sarah is that being wild and free isn't all about mustangs running down the beach and the wind blowing in my hair as I stare off into the sunset—a mighty warrior-princess of God. Sometimes, maybe most times, embracing wild and free is seizing the ability to be interrupted. God's version of wild and free looks like interruption to us because even the least organized of us have some preconceived picture of how our lives should and could go. But He is bigger, He is wilder, and His plan is better than we could ask or imagine.

And that is the truth about our God. Since the beginning of

mankind, we have expected Him to be like us, to be restrained or on the trajectory we're on, and He constantly breaks that mold and consistently stays God. Our Father was wild when He put Adam and Eve out of the garden and stood fiercely by His glory and His Word. But our great God was also wild when He didn't leave us on that path with that story. He was wild when He sent Jesus to live the life we couldn't and pay the price for our sins. Jesus was wild when He said, "I'm leaving, but I'm sending another—Holy Spirit! He'll sweep in and be your advocate."

Then there was the time when God told Abraham and Sarah they'd be the mother and father of a nation—though they were one hundred years old and ninety years old, respectively. It was wild beyond comprehension to send a baby to a poor teenager to be the King of kings and Lord of lords. As a murderer with a speech impediment, Moses would've been the most foolish choice to lead a nation, but our God is wild.

When He asked Noah to build a boat that would save a remnant of humankind from a flood, it had never rained. There was no rhythm or structure for how that would work, but it did. In the book of Joshua, our wild God gave humans the ability to stop the sun from going down. He paused the very system He created that sustains all of human life so a war could be won, because He's wild like that.

And here I sit. Really buying into the idea that it works best if women would read their Bible in the morning (as opposed to the afternoon) and feeling like things would go more smoothly if everyone would read the same devotional book—you know, so we can be on the same page. Worried that so-and-so might not have enough experience to lead other women and concerned that everyone else is not living the contained, small, me-serving life filled with the same rhythms and regulations.

I'm scared that the women coming behind me have seen the

absolute wrong picture. They've seen tidy and safe, and they've seen me worship a God who lives within my limitations and my spectrum of what is possible. I will get bold and ask God for things that serve my purposes as long as I can picture them actually happening, but rarely do I ask Him to step into my life and act like He normally acts—totally *not* like a human and fully like a wild Father who knows better.

Since I've had to confess to you that I don't always have a great track record of seeing and relating to a wild God, I also want to tell you about some other women. These gals have set their eyes on Him and let Him dictate what their lives look like, not their "limitations" or their preconceived notions and preferences.

I want to tell you about Jackie. Jackie was casually mentoring me for a season in Seattle, and my friend Annie and I would go drink coffee at her house and let our kids play together while she gave us sweet and sound biblical counsel. Jackie made me laugh, and she also set me seriously at ease. She spoke truth, but she poured on grace just like she'd pour honey into our coffee cups from her ginormous bulk honey jar. One day, when Annie had gone to her house but I couldn't, Jackie went to wake up her baby son, Zeke, from his nap. Devastatingly, she found him dead. Still. Inexplicably but assuredly in the arms of Jesus.

As I watched Jackie grieve over the next weeks and months, I could barely stand it. She didn't deserve that kind of pain, and Lord knows her family didn't either. But she woke up each day and went on with life, still moving forward and praising God. I'm sure it wasn't tidy, but to me it was heroic. Christ inside of her was so big and so strong, and yet I was knocked off my feet a few months later when I read something she wrote. She said that essentially she'd always asked for the Lord to keep her kids safe, and isn't that what He'd done? He'd brought Zekey home, safe to His arms. Jackie saw God outside of her own box and her own desires and saw

Him as bigger. And because of that, she could praise Him through devastation and continue asking Him to keep her kids safe.

I want to tell you about Connie. I first heard about Connie when we moved to Indiana for ministry. My husband would tell me about her and what a fiery pistol for Jesus she was. She loved reading, writing, and mostly ministering to the teenage Muslim community in our town. They were constantly in her home, eating her food and pouring out their hearts to her. On a side note, Connie is also a paraplegic. An assistant lives with her to take care of her, but I have never once seen her allow anything about her physical condition be a limitation for her and the great commission that is on her life.

I do think she's headstrong and brave, but mostly I think she has eyes to see how wild her God is. To me, she takes the Father at His Word when He says He can do something. When He says He loves her. When He says He has a plan for her. It seems like she believes her Father and His ability more than she believes in her own or in any lack of ability she might have. Her life is far from typical for a believing woman in her twenties or thirties, but it's rich beyond words, and it's wild and free because her Dad is.

I want to tell you about my own mom, who was a single mother in her thirties with two incredibly unruly girls who were going downhill fast. I want to tell you how she believed in God for more and continually prayed without ceasing that God would change our hearts and bring godly men to lead us. That hadn't been her initial story, but she didn't see her limitations as God's. Her heavenly Dad was wild; He could do what He wanted. She could ask for more than she could even imagine. My sister and I are both thankfully not in jail right now (though our behavior in high school certainly pointed to our eventually ending up there) but instead are married to two of the godliest men I know.

There are dozens of other women I want to tell you about, and

I wish I could sit in your house and hear your own story and see the threads of where God has been wild in your life too. But my encouragement to you is to run to the wild God and ask for eyes to truly see Him. Look for Him in the Word, and pray for a heart that is soft to perceive just how big He is. Read about the wild God who caused a flood to consume the earth when His beloved people went astray. Look full into the eyes of the same God who promised never to do it again, no matter how bad they got. Read John 2, where Jesus wildly turned water into wine at a wedding, not for the sake of intoxication but to proclaim His ability to miraculously perform wonders in the midst of the details. Open your heart and your eyes and take Him in—your wild God.

And then, sister, remember that He is working in the exact same way with the exact same wild power in your heart and life today. Right now. He is still as capable and as holy and as good as He ever was. Moreover, the same power that comes effortlessly to Him and allows Him to do whatever He wills for the sake of His glory is available to you through the power of the Holy Spirit. Wherever you are, whatever your circumstances—His arm is long, His love is great, and His ways are wild.

May you and I become more and more like Him.

PRAYER

Father, we want to say thank you for being the wild Creator. For being bigger and better than we could imagine, for being about Yourself and out for Your glory. Thank You for loving us ferociously and relentlessly for our good and the good of Your kingdom, and for defying our limited expectations of just how wild that love can be. Thank You for being wild even when we're small, and for being relentless in Your love even when we're restless and aren't doing our best to love You. Give us eyes to see and ears to hear and hearts that burn with praise and adoration and expectation that You will move freely in our lives.

HAYLEY'S RESPONSE

I'm the queen of the "yeah, but—" with God. I hope for the easy things, the well-defined-by-Scripture things, the things that are hard to be let down in. I don't get audacious very often. I rarely get the desperate kind of hopeful. The only-God-can-do-this kind of hopeful. I very much prefer to keep God in my own comfortable box and put Him on the shelf next to my favorite Bible. Important, but safe. Totally learnable, understandable, and not even a little wild. But how offensive is that to our infinite God?

God was never meant to be held back by our human allowances. He will not be contained or pacified. He will not be made smaller.

I think my feelings of being "too much" are from the same place that says "don't get too wild" when talking about God. But it's clear in Scripture that God does what He pleases and sets the rules. I don't know about you, but I'm learning to let go of convincing myself I already know what He's up to and what He's capable of. Because He just keeps surprising me at every turn.

The God of Freedom

In 2013, I hopped on an airplane with an eclectic group of women. Among us were a blogger who had traded her country life for inner-city ministry, an up-and-coming (now up-and-come) Christian music star, an elite fashion blogger, a chef to America's biggest celebrities, and a former bachelorette from ABC's hit reality show.

We met for the first time in person right before we got on a flight across the ocean. We quickly exchanged hugs of hello, grabbed some cellophane-wrapped airport sandwiches, and squeezed into our seats for the flight. We really had no idea what awaited us when we touched down on the other side of the world in Addis Ababa, Ethiopia.

We had been gathered to see firsthand the work of fashionABLE, an organization whose mission is to create sustainable business in Africa. We thought we were going to see how products were made and the ways the business was ethical, and to make sure the whole operation was on the up-and-up. We thought we were there to tell a good story so we could help fashionABLE sell more products and create more jobs.

However, on that trip I saw that the language of freedom crossed cultural lines.

I met a woman who had been told by her aunt that she was being shipped from her small rural town to the big city for the chance to go to school. However, instead of uniforms and fresh notebooks, she found herself trafficked into sex slavery. I met

83

another woman who had to leave her toddlers while they slept in an unsecured, tent-like shanty while she went to work in the sex industry at night because there was no one to watch her boys and she needed the money to support them.

I heard these stories, and it was like listening to a piece of investigative journalism from *60 Minutes*. It felt like a sweeping narrative of despair and then bondage, but the exciting part was that I also got to witness the joy on their faces when they expressed their release and rescue.

The crazy thing is, Scripture is full of stories of desperation and hope. Adam and Eve despaired, but God promised a coming hope. Israel was enslaved, but God set them free. Jesus died, but He rose again. When we despair and are enslaved, God says this will not be forever. He is in the business of setting people free. He opens cages and teaches us to fly.

And sure enough, God was about to bring hope the only way God can.

The women I met who worked in the sex industry were given a chance at another occupation through the work of fashionABLE, and their lives have been changed. Some of these brave women have chosen to write a short sentence or two describing their freedom story. This becomes part of fashionABLE's brand identity—the "Able Statement." On each fashionABLE product, there is a hand-written note to the purchaser that begins, "Because of you, I am able to _____." This amazing organization provides alternative employment to at-risk women, who are then able to find freedom from soul-crushing sex work.

The most poignant moment of that trip happened when our group traveled to a rural town outside of Addis Ababa. We were meeting with young women at the beginning of their lives outside of sex work or other at-risk situations. Their emotional wounds were still fresh, and I was more than a little nervous. I felt out of my comfort zone, having just bump, bump, bumped my way over the African soil in a van with two puking travel mates. I felt frazzled and overstimulated but so hopeful that God would show more of Himself than I'd seen before.

When we got there, we were greeted by these impossibly young women and a throng of giggling children. There was a palpable joy and peace, even amid the chaos and my own frayed nerves. We sat down in rows of folding chairs. Our translator (who was also their mentor and friend) introduced us to each other, and we started to share our stories. My favorite moment was when that up-and-coming Christian music star, Ellie Holcomb, got up and belted out a song she'd been fiddling around with before we left for the trip.

> Roll away this stone
> Roll away this sorrow
> And take away this pain
> That I've been holding on to, yeah
> 'Cause I want to be
> Like the birds all singing in the trees
> Oh, Lord, I want to be free
>
> So take away this fear
> Take away this doubting
> Let me know that You're here
> And You're not going anywhere, yeah
> 'Cause I want to be
> Like the fish all swimming in the sea
> Oh, Lord, I want to be free
> 'Cause I want to be
> Like the children playing in the breeze
> Oh, Lord, I want to be free
> Oh, my Lord, come and set us all free[7]

I recorded the song on my cell phone, and I still get goose-bumps when I play it back. The man translated the song to the young women after Ellie sang it, and it was apparent they'd heard the message loud and clear the first time. There were about eighty wet and sparkling eyes sitting row by row, just astounded at God's story of freedom.

I knew our eyes were leaking tears for different reasons. I sensed that the Ethiopian women were praising God for freeing them from physical bondage, that they were set on safe and solid ground. In my own heart, I was crying because I knew I was immensely blessed to be physically free and very privileged, but I didn't feel free deep in my spirit.

I'd left America for Ethiopia wondering what God was going to do with this trip. The trip happened during a very full season of my life. I'd given birth to our third little boy and launched The Influence Network in the seven months prior to getting on that airplane. The demands on my time, resources, and relationships were at a fever pitch. I knew there was more to life than more, more, more, but it was on that trip that God first started whispering freedom into the song of my life.

I feared discomfort more than I believed in God's power, and it was crippling me spiritually. I was starting to see the fruits of freedom wither on the vine of my life. The thing is, God is A-OK with discomfort and conflict; in fact, He confronts us all the time to get us to the point of repentance and reconciliation. This kindness is the gospel of freedom.

In our present culture, it can feel like it's every woman for herself. The needs of the many trump the needs of the one. Our capitalist society is all about efficiency, the bottom line, and the lowest cost. But in God's economy, there is no lack in His resources, and it means He is extravagant and free to give.

The Freest Feeling in the World

Physical bondage is a scary reality for many women in the world—as my new Ethiopian friends had experienced. In fact, in my own little suburban county, women were being trafficked through a massage parlor, with vanloads of new women coming every day. They were incredibly vulnerable, spoke no English, and were entrapped in every way. Seeing disenfranchised women, you can see they lack so much, but so many of the women I met in Ethiopia shone brightly in the light of Jesus. Their lack had brought them closer to the Lord.

Most of us are not subject to physical bondage, and for that I'm out-of-my-mind grateful. But the forces of darkness still try to bind us to something to keep us from bonding to God. In Jesus' famous Sermon on the Mount, He outlined the ways His followers would be blessed. Matthew 5:3 recounts Him saying, "Blessed are the poor in spirit," and I really believe that. Sometimes I wonder if our privilege keeps us from experiencing the true soul freedom God has for us.

The women I know are not physically bound or materially lacking, but I'll tell you what I see every day. I see that we're living in a fallen world. I see that our hopes and expectations are falling short. I see broken relationships and shattered families. I see that we need freedom from sin, believing that the Holy Spirit will grow every good fruit in us. I see that we need to throw off the self-imposed limitations we've collected through defensive living. I see that we need freedom from shame; we need to hold true to the promises of God and fling the rest far away.

God has called you beloved. He is the giver of every good gift. He has promised you a Counselor who will cause your life to bloom and explode with good fruit. He has told you that if you know His Son, you are free. He has promised that He is making all things new again. He's a gracious and generous giver who has already made a way. He's illuminated a path to freedom, and it's through Jesus. That's such good news.

Our life in Jesus means we're made righteous and have no need for shame or fear of sin. Our life in the Spirit means our life will bear good fruit. Our life with the Father means we're just where we should be, created with love for a good purpose.

Two parables in the book of Luke strike me because they show just how generous and gracious God is. Because God is freedom, He can freely give. Our freedom is found in Him, and it's an unearned grace. Oftentimes I think people fear freedom because it might lead us to stray from the good path. I think our churches sometimes unintentionally teach us this. When I was a new believer, I felt incredibly grateful for the gift of salvation. It felt mystical and beautiful and almost impossible. I knew I was saved from my past. However, I soon picked up—through words spoken and unspoken—that I'd better be good from now on. I'd better not topple off the high wire, because I'd already used up my one "get out of jail free" card.

I wish I'd understood then what I know to be true now: *I was saved for eternity once, but this good news still applies to me every single day.* God's power works in my life every day. He's pursuing me still. I still sin, and He's still rescuing me. The good news still changes my life every single day. These parables in Luke helped me hop off the high wire and take a deep breath.

When we begin reading Luke 15, the Pharisees and the tax collectors are gathering around Jesus. These folks seem like the most graceless people around, right? They're all policies and regulations. They'd be massively concerned with efficiencies and economies of scale and return on investment. They'd be the ones to point out wastefulness and disorganization. If nothing else, they'd want to make sure every box was checked and every rule was followed.

Well, it's no surprise that Jesus was about to preach some parables that were lush with extravagance. This extravagance isn't wasteful to God, though. Remember, God's pockets are bottomless, so care is never wasted when it is expended. The Pharisees and tax collectors probably thought Jesus was unwise, naive about business, and certainly not fit to be a leader.

Jesus began talking about the lives of a flock of sheep and their shepherd—imagery that is thick throughout the Bible. He pointedly asked the gathered rule followers, "Suppose one of you has a hundred sheep and loses one of them. Doesn't he leave the ninety-nine in the open country and go after the lost sheep until he finds it?"

I can imagine the way this came across to the people who had gathered to listen to Jesus. Their jobs required them to be particular and to keep score. I wonder if they felt like it would be wise to go with the sure bet of ninety-nine sheep rather than risk the rest scattering while the shepherd searched for the one. I know that would be my temptation. I'd probably spout something off like, "Well, you can't win 'em all" and secretly feel pretty smug with my ninety-nine well-behaved sheep. I'd probably think that particular lost sheep was always the troublemaker anyway—just a lost cause. I'd probably start thinking back to the past times that sheep had offended me, looking for justification for leaving her behind.

But here's what a shepherd would know. Sheep have been completely domesticated, and their way of defensive living is "safety in numbers." So they learn from birth to stick together and actually feel insecure without each other. Those ninety-nine other sheep would stick together. But that one sheep out wandering alone, that sheep is as good as dead. She is likely highly agitated, unaware of her surroundings, and completely frightened, even though she willfully wandered off.

So Jesus talks about the shepherd who goes and fetches the lost sheep. He calls out to the sheep, and the sheep recognizes his voice (John 10:27). When he finally finds that lost little lamb, he cries out with excitement and hoists the sheep onto his shoulders. He carries that lamb to safety and back to the flock.

The shepherd finds those who have wandered off, who have always been a little unruly, and joyfully brings them home. There was never a worry for the ninety-nine, because those ninety-nine had each other. That one sheep, even if she did it to herself, was lost, afraid, and alone. But the shepherd went to fetch her and bring her back to himself.

Reading this parable makes me feel brave. Because we never need to be afraid of failure—not when God's grace will always be there to break our fall. It makes me not fear accidentally wandering off the right path. I know we have a Shepherd who will come and look for us. His worry is not for the many in the flock who needn't repent, but for the one who has gone astray. We can follow Him with abandon, never worrying that in following Him we'll go the wrong way! We can follow Him in freedom, because His love is so freely given.

But if this parable felt lavish, get ready to be dazzled by the next parable. It's one of the most preached-on parables in Scripture for good reason. It is truly stunning, both in the story arc and in the rich theology it contains.

In Luke 15:11–32, we read about a family of boys. If there is one thing I know, it's families of boys. I grew up with all brothers, and I'm in the midst of raising four sons. I am fluent in the way of boys. There is an understood order of things, and each brother grows into his place in the family. There is some jockeying for position. Knowing this, it's not shocking to me that the boys in Luke 15 are polar opposites in personality.

First, let's talk about the younger brother. He got impatient and wanted his inheritance right away. So his father gave it to him, and the younger brother left the family and set off to create his own success and live his own way. He moved far away from the family and promptly spent everything he had. I imagine he spent some money on a nice apartment, maybe took a vacation to rest up from the big move, and then probably squandered the rest on little luxuries like Starbucks and trips to Target (is that just me?).

Unfortunately, hard times hit, and he found himself in need. He had nothing to eat, and one day, he realized he was enviously eyeing some animal feed. That moment woke him right up. He realized that because he had wanted so badly to strike out on his own, he was now hungry and without hope. He remembered what the servants in his father's house ate, and it was certainly better than any of his current options.

So he decided it was time to patch things up with his dad. He knew how much he had offended his father, and he knew he could only ever ask to be allowed back into the family home as a hired hand. But he hoped if he begged for forgiveness from God and from his father, then maybe his father would allow him to work in the house they used to share.

I can certainly understand that. When I've royally screwed up, I never want to expect full forgiveness and complete restoration to my previous position. I want to ask for just the most meager portion of forgiveness because it feels less risky on my part. Maybe I feel I don't really deserve freedom, or maybe I'm content with a pittance. But I've learned this is not the way of God.

It's illustrated in this parable just how freely God gives grace. When we get to the bottom of ourselves and our ability to provide, we get to a place of need, which is the only place we'll be able to accept grace.

The boy's father spotted him while he was still far away. He ran out of the house and was practically frantic with excitement. His boy had come home, and the father was filled with compassion. He wrapped his son in a warm hug, which I'm sure made the young man squirmy. There's something about free and extravagant grace that is initially uncomfortable. It requires an immense amount of humility and a gracious thank you.

But the father didn't accept his son's plea to be a hired servant. He ordered his servants to get the boy's best belongings and restore them to him. Then they had a massive feast to celebrate the son who was as good as dead but had returned. I can just imagine that party—under the stars, twinkly lights casting a beautiful glow, a soundtrack of joyful music, and so much laughter. In the movie in my mind, there is beautiful B-roll footage of people hugging and dancing, eyes glittering with hope and reconciliation.

That's the crazy thing. Reconciliation feels so good once you're on the other side. The repentance part feels hard, but God freely welcomes us back with open arms.

That's what freedom feels like.

But let's look at another character in the story who shows us what life looks like when we're missing this kind of freedom.

The person I ache for most in this scenario is the older brother. I see so much of myself in him, and, honestly, for a long time I totally missed the fact that this parable illuminates the goodness of God as our redeemer and the grace that is freely given. I felt anger on behalf of the older brother, knowing full well I would have been him. I imagine that the Pharisees and tax collectors listening to Jesus tell this story would have also acted like the older brother.

He was such a classic older brother. He did what he was told. He was loyal. He was careful and measured. He dotted his i's and crossed his t's perfectly and harbored pride in that fact. My guess is that he resented his little brother's flakiness long before the little brother ever left the family home. When he left and squandered his wealth and word got back to the family, I imagine the older brother thought, *Well, he sure got what he deserved. He was always a little punk.*

The older brother certainly did not respond graciously to his younger brother, but he also became angry with his father. He hated the free grace his father gave his screwed-up little brother. He listed all the ways *he'd* followed the rules with his father—and also how his father had never rewarded him for it.

But what the father said next really sticks with me. He essentially said, "Yes. You *have* always been good and loyal. You *have* never left my side. But that's the goodness of it—not the fattened calf, not the party, but that we've always been together. I was always in your presence, and you in mine. We had communion with each other, but we didn't have that with your little brother. Now we can celebrate the goodness of his return and can all be reconciled to each other."

God is freedom. He freely gives to all of us. He gives of Himself most of all, and that is the prize. Sometimes it feels like the prodigal son, the little brother, got a larger portion of God's good stuff. But the reality is, the older brother always had the father. He always had the chance to enjoy relationship together. That is always, always the prize. So in that regard, the older brother was already enjoying his inheritance.

But even in that confrontation with his father, he had his own bit of disruption in the relationship, which will probably drive him to repentance and his own moment of total understanding of grace. He will get to reconcile with his father and see how much his father wants that reconciliation and relationship. Knowing that you can never break things beyond repair is the freest feeling in the world.

These two parables shock me in the lavish freedom they offer us. We know we will always be fought for, always be wanted, and always be seen. The fact that we can't screw it all up with God allows me to freely live. And these are not the only two abundant examples of grace in Scripture. The whole sweeping arc of the Bible is a great story of God seeking out the sinner and making a way for her through the cross of Christ. Of setting the captives free. Of rescuing the vulnerable from the oppressor and releasing us from our own mistakes and failures.

> For Christ's love compels us, because we are convinced that one died for all, and therefore all died. And he died for all, that those who live should no longer live for themselves but for him who died for them and was raised again.
>
> So from now on we regard no one from a worldly point of view. Though we once regarded Christ in this way, we do so no longer. Therefore, if anyone is in Christ, the new creation has come: The old has gone, the new is here! All this is from God, who reconciled us to himself through Christ and gave us the ministry of reconciliation: that God was reconciling the world to himself in Christ, not counting people's sins against them. And he has committed to us the message of reconciliation. We are therefore Christ's ambassadors, as though God were making his appeal through us. We implore you on Christ's behalf: Be reconciled to God. God made him who had no sin to be sin for us, so that in him we might become the righteousness of God.
>
> *2 Corinthians 5:14–21*

The old has gone, the new is here! What incredibly good news! God is freedom. We cannot be free without him, but in Him we are truly free.

All of Scripture is a sweeping story of God righting wicked systems, setting people free, and making Himself known to a world that needs Him. His Word makes His character and promises clear to us.

Come into the Light

God's freedom goes all the way back to the beginning. God was not created, but He was before all things. This was the hardest thing for me to grasp as a child, even before I believed in God as a Father and Jesus as a Savior. I would always wonder, *But who created God?* Because everything on earth has come from God, it is hard to believe that God didn't originate from someone or something else. This is powerful, if you think about it, because every other thing that has existed in history was a created thing. It was conceived or built or fashioned out of something that already existed before that. Except for God.

God was here before it all. He is free because there is no one above Him. He submits to no one and is mastered by no one. God sets the tone, and the whole earth follows. He set the stars in the sky and separated day and night, just as He does darkness from light. He is not mastered by the limits of time. His days do not look like ours, governed by the tick of the clock.

God is not mastered by His means, because His storehouses are overflowing and He gives with abandon. He doesn't know lack or plenty; He only knows infiniteness.

God is all-encompassing, all-consuming, and mighty, and He is the solution to defensive living. He pulls us under His wing and protects us. He becomes our armor, allowing us to let down our self-made defenses. He has already equipped us for every situation we find ourselves in. If we were made in the image of this mighty God, why do we shirk away, afraid we aren't enough or maybe even too much? We can't go anywhere where He is not already. We cannot outpace Him, because He is already there.

> Where can I go from your Spirit?
> Where can I flee from your presence?

> If I go up to the heavens, you are there;
>> if I make my bed in the depths, you are there.
> If I rise on the wings of the dawn,
>> if I settle on the far side of the sea,
> even there your hand will guide me,
>> your right hand will hold me fast.
>
> *Psalm 139:7–10*

God is beholden only to the promises He Himself has made. The one thing is, God cannot contradict Himself. He is good and cannot ever in any single moment be anything other than good. He is strong and mighty, and his purposes will prevail (Proverbs 19:21). He made promises to Noah and to Abraham and to all Israel, and He has made promises to us today.

He has promised we'll inherit His freedom when we know Jesus. Like the prodigal son, we have a Father who is willing to give us part of our inheritance *now*. Our freedom is passed down through His Son, Jesus.

God is in control of everything but doesn't manipulate us like puppets. He sees all and knows all, but He also allows us to make decisions. We have the agency of free will, and He will not control us like pawns. We are not tools in His tool belt; we are dearly loved daughters set free by His Son.

God does not worry; He is peace. There is no fear in Him. He is love, and perfect love drives out all fear. We are released from a life of anxiety, because He's asked us to cast our cares on Him. He bears up under the weight of our worry, and He says His yoke is easy.

God forgives and brings all things to the light. God has forgiven us, and He exhorts us to be in the light "as he is in the light" (1 John 1:7). He is standing there in the light waiting for you. The best part about bringing things to the light is that He is already there, ready to be with you and convict you and comfort you. He is not afraid of confrontation, because it is often conflict that draws people out of hiding and into the light.

When I play back that video of Ellie singing in a bright room in Ethiopia, I feel hope. I feel a reminder of the first ripples of the song of freedom in my life. I know I am free, and I want it for other women. I want it for women who are in physical bondage, and I want it for women who are slaves to expectations, fear, sin, and shame.

I can't help but feel relief and gratefulness that the gospel ties us together and gives us freedom. I believe that we, like the prodigal son, will experience restoration and lavish grace. When we submit ourselves to God, it feels like a weight is lifted and things are back in balance. We are no longer trying to maintain control and comfort, but we rely on God's saving and sustaining goodness to be our all. We lay down our defensive living and allow Him to be our provider and our protector.

PRAYER

Heavenly Father, You are freedom in all of the best ways. You were there before anything had shape or form. Your love is so full of freedom—so ridiculously lavish and unconditional. Lord, thank You for being the Father to the prodigals who are lost, as well as to the older brothers and sisters who think they've got it all figured out. Thank You for offering us the prize of relationship with You. Thank You for taking off all the worldly markings of success and pushing us back to Jesus' work on the cross as a reminder of Your goodness. We're grateful that You're not bound by time or people. We're grateful You're only bound by what You say to be true of Yourself and by Your promises. Thank You for that. Help us to believe it.

JESS'S RESPONSE

Reading Hayley's words makes me want to ask, "Am I living free? Have I forgotten all this freedom that's been purchased for me?" There is something about this kind of liberty that's slightly uncomfortable—it feels like free falling. But I'm ready to jump. I don't want to find myself waiting inside the chains of my own man-made safety when all this freedom is waiting for me. I'm recommitting again and reminding myself of this truth: Contained, domesticated, terrified living is not the kind of life Christ died for me to live.

Our Eden Identity: Created as Wild and Good

The word *good* is so overused—and even misused—in our culture today that it's hard to know what it even means anymore. Think about it. When you cross paths on your way to the bathroom at church. When you bump into your girlfriend at the gym. As you're passing by in your car, windows rolled down in the preschool pickup line. Someone asks how you're doing, and you respond as you're expected to: "Good. You?"

If you're like me, you keep the permasmile on long enough to turn the corner or get to the bathroom, or you wait at least till you're out of earshot to return to whatever it was you were genuinely feeling. Maybe you were in the middle of fussing at your kids or tugging at your shirt because it was clinging funny. Perhaps you were blinking back tears and just trying to make it to a safe place where you could cry in peace. Maybe you actually feel amazing, but you know it's better to keep your incredibly good news inside rather than blabbing it all around and having people think you're bragging. The point is, we rarely feel simply "good," and yet that's the declaration we live under. We feel there's no other socially acceptable answer to society's favorite question: "How are you?"

I'm afraid we've made *good* so casual, so misunderstood, that we need to go back to the beginning to remember what it really means.

What happened to the women of God, the daughters who were pronounced "good" by their Abba, not on the basis of their circumstances but the identity of their Creator? It feels highly unlikely that you'd ask a friend how she's doing and she'd spit back some honest and heartfelt theology about how good her God is and therefore just how at ease she feels herself.

Here is how Genesis describes the creation of mankind: "Then God said, 'Let us make mankind in our image, in our likeness, so that they may rule over the fish in the sea and the birds in the sky, over the livestock and all the wild animals, and over all the creatures that move along the ground.' So God created mankind in his own image, in the image of God he created them; male and female he created them" (Genesis 1:26–27).

Have you ever seen one of those time lapses of the earth changing? Flowers pushing up, mountains pushing apart and back together again, seas receding and joining? I pray that when we get the big tour around eternity, we get to stand and watch a life-size time lapse of what it looked like when God created the earth. It's literally impossible to picture since we can't picture nothingness. But first, there was just Him. And then what? A spark? A fire? A flash? A small ball that appeared and rolled around, gaining mass and ground until it resembled the earth? Can you visualize it? Darkness, void, and blank—and then suddenly *light*. Life. Meaning. Existence.

I could study the Hebrew language of Genesis 1 for months on end if I had the time. Verse 2 describes the earth as "formless," using the Hebrew word *tohu*, which means "unreality, emptiness, waste." The Hebrew unpacks even more in its description of the Spirit of God "hovering" (the Hebrew word is *rachaph*, meaning "flutter, move, shake, relax") over the waters, telling us that our triune God was present in tender love, relaxing in the void as He did his fashioning and framing. Let your imagination run wild with me for a moment. When we picture the particles coming together to form rocks and soil and the wings of birds, we can see Him. In our mind's eye, as we're watching Him casually point to where the oceans will stop, we can worship. As we see Him effortlessly adjust the tilt of the earth to exactly the right angle so we don't fall off into the universe, we can just breathe a sigh of praise and relief.

And as God moved and created and formed, as He brought meaning and life and something where there was nothing, He called it good. *Tob* is the Hebrew word our Father used when it was all finished. *Tob* is another rich word with several meanings: "beautiful, pleasant, rich, better, best." Isn't it amazing to think that we spend so much of our lives on this quest for the best when God has already declared it of us, His workmanship—*the best*? As He created, He declared things *tob. Light, good. Darkness, good. Land, good. Air, good. Sea, good. Animals, good. Man, good. Woman, good.* I love the word *tob.* I love to tell it to other women. I like the way it sounds on my tongue. I love what it means for me. *Good.* There is no confusion or doubt or fear—just good.

My second favorite Hebrew word in the whole Old Testament is found in Genesis 2:7. *Yatsar* is the word used to describe specifically how God "formed" mankind, and it's a delicate and specific word. The literal translation refers to a potter fashioning something out of clay, and, goodness gracious, that makes me feel known and seen. The Father, who had only just a little earlier created light without blinking an eye or feeling any stress, created humans intricately and creatively, like an artist. His brow was not furrowed in fear or confusion as He crafted us. It was with joy, with ease, with flourish, with tenderness that He intricately designed us in His image.

If God, in all of His holiness and perfection, has handcrafted you and created you, dreamed you up and set you apart, called you into service and ambassadorship, and placed you at His right hand—with your co-heir and brother, Christ—then who are you to say you are not good? Who are you to call any part of what He has made bad? Your personality, body, gifts, dreams, voice, story, ideas, passions, family, and convictions—where in Scripture do you find any authority to see those as anything but God-given and God-approved?

When we critique ourselves or discount ourselves, we are doing the very opposite of worship. When we pinch our thighs in disgust, when we shake our heads at how awkward we feel, when we stand in the mirror and look on in frustration, when we look to the right or the left and assume that everything would be better if we just had that one person's life, gift, beauty, talent, family, or home, we are not in agreement with our Father, who has made us, appointed us, and called it all *good*.

We are flat-out telling God He is wrong.

Let's put that aside now. Let's move forward in this agreement: What God has called good, we will no longer call anything else.

I've never gotten into pottery, but over the years, I've come to accept that God made me to be an artist, and so I do that. For fun, for business, for myself and others—I make art. Nothing makes me feel more at home than listening to loud music as I sling paint and try to pour out some emotions and thoughts through colors instead of words. But here's the deal: I don't always like the art I make. I don't think that everything I do is beautiful. I throw drafts away; I paint over mistakes; and I am capable of making some pretty ugly junk any day of the week.

For a long time, I read the creation story as if God were like me, and that is not a wise thing to do. I imagined Him walking (floating? soaring? gliding?) around the earth, making things and gazing on them and saying, "Oh, that's good! I like that one!" I don't think that's wrong, but I don't think it's the full picture either.

The full picture, you see, requires you and me to acknowledge that the main character of the story is not the masterpiece, but its Creator.

You and I are created *good*. But without God, we aren't good or holy.

It is these two truths together that make the full picture of who we are and who God is.

When our eyes are on God and His goodness, we can rightly worship. When our eyes are on ourselves, we see only our own insufficiencies. Because God is the essence of good, He is incapable of creating anything but good. With God, there are no castoffs. There are also no favorites. There are only masterpieces—every single time.

We could read Scripture and see that God calls us good, stick it in our pocket, take it home, and try to believe it. We can try daily to put that truth on and believe it with all our might. But it's incredibly hard, right? Because we *know* us. More than anyone else, I know the hurt I can cause. I know my sin is rampant most days, and I've heard the thoughts in my head that would terrify others because they're so incredibly sinful. When my eyes are on me, it's ridiculously difficult to believe I am anything good.

The other option is, as wild women of God, to ask for eyes to see that the main character of this story is our Father—relaxed and at ease, not striving or fearful of what is going to come of His production. Holy and perfect. Creative and intentional. Artistic and almighty. And like when we read a book from a different perspective, we can really hear what His voice sounded like when it declared all that He'd made to be *good*.

It was with authority. It was with composure. It was worshipful, not of the creation, but of His own glorious nature. Not, "Oh look! This is good, right?" but, "Good. Of course, good. Only good. Because all that I am is good." When the Creator declares the quality of creation, it's not for the affirmation of the creature but for the praise of His glorious and intrinsic goodness.

And all of this matters because today, where you sit, you are still that creation He calls good. Not because you've done anything to earn it, but because you were made in the very image of the God of all good.

You may be raising an eyebrow right now. You may be thinking, *Hold on, Jess. I feel like anything but a good masterpiece at this moment.* So where is this disconnect coming from? If we're so "good," why do we feel so battered and bruised sometimes?

To be honest, I feel exactly the same way.

Getting Back to Good

I have a serious confession, ladies.

I am the most obnoxious morning person you'll ever meet.

If you happen to meet me between the hours of 9:00 a.m. and 8:00 p.m., you'll find a semi-agreeable and normal human. I'm not overly peppy, and I don't think too many people would find me disagreeable. However, between the hours of 5:00 a.m. and 9:00 a.m., you might find my optimism and excited disposition downright annoying if you don't have a matching personality. I want to talk, I want to cuddle or hug, and I might just bust out some of my best high-pitched noises to communicate. Because I *love* mornings.

But here's what most people don't know: I become a shell of a human after 8:00 p.m. I'm too tired to talk, can't form complete sentences, don't really have a lot of energy to do anything, and, in general, my hopeful disposition is gone. And it's not just because I get up too early—I think it's honestly because I really struggle with what goes on in my heart throughout the day.

I wake hopeful and abounding in faith of what God might do that day. Something stirring in my heart really believes Ephesians 3:20—that He is going to do immeasurably more than I could ask or imagine. And He does! He always does. Every single day. He never fails to show up and move and shift things in the kingdom of God as my human day goes by. But you know what doesn't go as well as I hope, ever? Me. It's not like I wake up every day assuming I won't sin, but just as I hope in the Lord, I find myself putting hope in my own self and being let down every single day.

Guys, this weird thing happens—and I. Just. Keep. Sinning. Pride, selfishness, anger—they shift, and the Lord grows me, and sometimes the issues dissipate, but they're all still there. And what's more? I never seem to be able to get it all done. Even when I have a perfect plan and His holy help, it just doesn't happen. Then you add in other people and the little hurts and cuts and bruises that come from living with other broken humans day in and day out, and when it's all said and done, I'm toast. The shiny blank slate of my day is dashed because once again, I've been too much and—as always—I am never enough.

So almost every single night of my life, I lie in bed and let the day flash in my mind. *What happened? What didn't get done? How did I feel? How did I make others feel?* I measure myself against my own perceptions of what I think I should be, and in defeat I just hand it all back to Jesus. I ask Him to cover it with grace and help me again tomorrow. I am comforted by my Father, but I am rarely comfortable in my own flesh at the end of the day. It is at this point that I forget God has created me as "good." I forget, and it's easy—if I'm not careful—to let the focus shift back to myself.

Because I know all of our struggles are different, I asked several other women to describe the ways they live feeling less than "good" in their own skin every day, and here's what they said:

- "I automatically apologize when someone runs into my cart at Target or steps in front of me, even though I wasn't at fault. I think it's a matter of uneasiness and avoiding conflict."
- "I overexplain. I will say the same statement four or five different ways, address every emotion I didn't mean behind my statement. Just so I know I'm not offending anyone. Half the time I forget what I was even talking about and have to apologize for rambling."
- "I don't feel at ease because I constantly feel behind in life. When I compare my life stage to other women, I think something must be inherently wrong with me that I don't have the things they have or live the way they do."
- "I feel uneasy when I disagree with people or have to walk through conflict. Even if deep in my heart I know I believe or feel something strongly, it doesn't sit well with me when I'm opposing someone somehow with my own thoughts or opinions."
- "I consistently worry I'm not loving people enough or making them feel comfortable."
- "I feel completely uncomfortable when my weaknesses are exposed, and even more so when they affect other people. I know my husband knows I'm weak, but when it affects his day or his life, I feel broken."

It's one thing to feel convicted and broken over our sin and to put our hope in Christ to redeem our brokenness and grow us. But I find that many of us women are fighting an entirely different battle in that we are living lives of utter uneasiness. Even in the safety of Christian community, we are not comfortable with who we are.

So what has happened? Why do we feel so far from that pro-nouncement of good that God made at the beginning? We know He is infinitely majestic and worthy of worship. By association, we as His creations were initially established as good because our God cannot, in His perfect nature, make things that are busted or flawed. But then what? Eve ate the fruit—and the fall happened, and thousands of years of crippling sin hit our species. Death and destruction entered in, and our earth got a new, temporary prince who seems to be able to break the good things and send culture to hell in a handbasket. Are we still good? Shouldn't we feel broken and scared and insecure about our standing because we *are* sinful and we *do* mess things up?

A pastor friend of mine bumped right into the answer—embarrassingly—in an important job interview at a church. The church leadership asked him to share the gospel. Simple, to the point. A bunch of pastors simply asking another pastor to recite the story we all know by heart. He started at creation and gave a beautiful biblical history about our Father, the people of God in the Old Testament, the prophets, and then on into the early church. He talked of our role in the body of believers now and how God was going to make all things new again, and he even dipped a little bit into Revelation. It was awesome. He did great. But as he finished and sat back in his chair, the other pastors chuckled a little and told him there was only one problem: He had totally forgotten Jesus.

And we're just like him. We forget Jesus. Just like we are not haphazardly good, we are not haphazardly covered in the blood of our Savior and made new. You and I, by grace through faith, are absolutely still right back in the same standing where we began: good. We are still 100 percent human and at the same time 100 percent forgiven and brought near to our perfect and holy Father. That word in Genesis used by the Creator to describe all that He'd made, including us? *Tob*. It means so many wonderful things: "good, better, best." But it also means "at ease."

The world is telling us that if we finally find who we're supposed to be, we'll be at ease. The world says you are good "if . . ."—but God says you are good, *period*. Once we identify our strengths and minimize our weaknesses, we'll be at ease. If we can reach a certain life stage or bank account amount, we can feel at ease. Maybe if we wait until we're in our thirties or forties or fifties or nineties, we'll discover what really matters and finally feel content with who we are. The world tells us that if we stay inside the lines—or if we color outside of them beautifully enough—we'll feel at ease. If we were in community more—or if we spent more time alone—we might feel more secure. Yoga might help or drinking more water or making a cleaning checklist.

What if you tried serving or getting up an hour earlier or reading that self-help book or trying that new face wash? Then, finally, one day, you might be your own self—radiant, at ease, best, better, beautiful.

But Jesus says no. You are not "too much" for His love and grace, and you have never been "not enough" for His affection and devotion. It isn't your goodness that drew Him to you, and God's love isn't dependent on your ability to stay inside the lines and hold it all together. He didn't just happen to cover your sin. He went to earth on a mission, spurred on by the great love and glory of your heavenly Father, and His death was not in vain. Our Savior paid the ultimate price so we could live the way we were intended to—underneath the banner of the gospel, at ease. And that is the truth we are called to walk in today.

You can stop running, stop striving, stop hoping that one day you'll be the better or best version of yourself. You can walk away from comparison, throw shame in the trash, and stop skipping around worrying about whose toes you step on. Because of Jesus, we don't have to try so hard. And we certainly don't need to fear being too much or not enough. We get to partner with Him in our lives, and that is good news, but nothing will fall or break or completely crumble when you rest. You are at ease in Christ, made new.

You Are Appointed for Good

The apostle Paul writes, "We are God's handiwork, created in Christ Jesus to do good works, which God prepared in advance for us to do" (Ephesians 2:10).

Not only are we identified supremely as "good" by God, but there's even more. Our divine *identity* as good propels us forward into the *mission* of good. We are not just created as good; we are appointed to do good. The richness of the Hebrew word *tob* doesn't just mean "good, better, best, and at ease." When used as a noun and not an adjective, it means "a benefit." Likewise, as daughters of God who are redeemed in Christ, we're not just ornaments to sit pretty on a shelf. We are pronounced as having purpose, conceived with an objective, given gifts and callings, and put on earth to help move the kingdom of God forward.

In chapter 1, we addressed the truth that we're no longer tools, but treasures of God, and this fact remains. The temptation is to lose the focus of the story or forget the posture of our heavenly Father toward us. It's easy to spin and toil and feel like we need to do more for the kingdom—to fulfill our purpose and to get done what it is that God has called us to. And where does that leave us? For me, it finds me back in bed at the end of the day, still feeling as if I am not enough or am missing it. It does not leave me feeling wild, and it does not incite freedom in my heart.

But we know better now, right? Let's realign our hearts and shake our heads and look at it again. Who is the main character in this whole shebang? God. Father. Abba and Holy Spirit and Jesus Christ, completely united and softly moving over all creation. Doing everything for their own glory but still loving us lavishly and with abandon. Moreover, they hold the entire universe in their hands. Not just all of our lives and hopes and dreams, but they hold all of the cards. There is nothing the triune God needs, and nothing He doesn't have dominion over.

And I'm wondering, *Do you still feel God is needing something from you? Is He waiting for you to get it all together or do it right? Is His kingdom dependent on your obedience or your performance? Is He surprised or let down by your constant humanness?* Absolutely not.

Ladies, when we flip the script and remember who the main character is, it takes the pressure off us. We get to lay down that burden of getting it right, because God's already got this—completely. It's not that we *have* to live for God; it's that we *get* to live for God. It's not that we *have* to serve Him; it's that we *get* to serve Him. It's not that He wants more *from* us; it's that He wants more *for* us.

You are the real work, and it is already finished. God does not need you to do something big for Him, and He doesn't need you to fulfill your part. But in His great love, He has prepared works for you, according to Ephesians 2:10, and He intentionally crafted you with gifts because He wants that life of giving and serving *for* you. He knows you're the most you when you're living out the calling He has given you. He knows the enemy is quieted when your loving is loud. He knows the ache that wonders what on earth you're here for. He's already prepared all of that and made a way, through the power of the Holy Spirit, for you to walk with Him *and* serve Him.

You are not a tool but a treasure. You are not a pawn but an appointed ambassador of a holy nation. Once you've tasted God's vision of wild and free, you begin to feel the urgency of His call to something more. God is on a mission to stage a kingdom-size wild and free takeover, and you are invited to be part of this good work.

One of the best parts is that we are in this together—a whole sisterhood of women called to roll up our sleeves. The Bible shows us what happens when women reclaim their identity as good and their mission to do good. Mary broke into song in Luke 1, crying out, "My soul glorifies the Lord and my spirit rejoices in God my Savior, for he has been mindful of the humble state of his servant. From now on all generations will call me blessed, for the Mighty One has done great things for me—holy is his name" (verses 46–49). I love thinking about Rahab the prostitute, who hid the men of God in her home and didn't seem to bat an eyelash at performing the duty that would ultimately betray her city and rulers. Her eyes weren't on herself, concluding how she couldn't possibly be right for the job—her eyes were on the God of Abraham, Isaac, and Jacob. The same God who was melting hearts in fear all around Rahab (Joshua 2:11).

Can you picture them in heaven—the great crowd of sister witnesses cheering you on? Eve. Sarah. Mary. Rahab. Deborah. Abigail. Anna. Leah. Lydia. Rachel. Ruth. Martha. Hagar. Esther. Tabitha. Zipporah. One by one, hundreds by hundreds, thousands by thousands. Lining eternity, ever worshiping—and cheering *you* on. They have the blessed viewpoint of knowing what's really important in the end, and they want you to keep your eyes on the prize. I have a feeling that if they could paint signs to hold up and cheer you on as you run this race of life, one might read, "You're already good! You're good because He's good! Worship Him and keep going!"

Sisters, we don't just have a beautiful inheritance as chosen princesses of a powerful and holy King. We have new identities— new, unchanging, re-created identities in which we've been called good. Not out of our own merit or anything we can earn or lose, but as an extension of the grace and perfection of our Father. We've been created intentionally and told we can be at ease, not striving or toiling or spinning, not continually looking behind us or apologizing as we go. Moreover, we've been given purpose and calling and equipped with individualized gifts for our specified areas of the kingdom of God. We are not trapped in broken identities or expectations. We are wild and free. We are good.

We've never been too much, and we are already enough. We are good with God because we are His daughters. We are good mothers. We are good sisters and friends and daughters. We are good workers. We are good lovers. We are good servants and helpers. We are not low or high on any totem pole—success, beauty, likeability, or any other characteristic. We have been called good by God, and *that* is how we find ourselves—because we believe Him. And anyway, it's about *His* glory, not ours.

PRAYER

Father, will You help us to rub in this truth and walk in the identity You've given us, not the busted one we've crafted for ourselves and learned to settle for? Will You speak the truth of who we are and whose we are deep into our hearts so we can move forward—on purpose, redeemed, and running wild and free? We love You.

HAYLEY'S RESPONSE

Gosh, I feel like I'm always longing to feel "at ease," and sometimes I think I feel homesick for heaven. I was just talking with my husband, Mike, about how when I turned thirty a couple weeks ago, I felt like it was this deadline for being the "Best Hayley." I needed to get my junk together and be a good exerciser, a great organizer, and the best housekeeper. I thought I needed those abilities to really be at ease with myself at thirty.

But it's good to know that part of this longing is because God has already called us *tob*. Our identity as we were created is to be at ease, and I for one am all about claiming that identity. It's something to walk in, not something to strive for.

Our Redeemed Identity: Re-created as Free

When Mike and I lived in Charlotte, we went to a church that identified itself as "a place for people who'd given up on church but not on God." It was the perfect place for two try-hard young adults to land. We moved to the area and started attending right after they built their first building and attendance exploded. We were still newlyweds; I was newly pregnant; and we had moved six hundred miles away from anyone who knew our names.

We had been good youth group kids who hadn't gotten into much trouble in life. It's hard to feel the weight of your sin when you haven't lived much life. So while we were skilled at playing by unspoken Christian culture rules, we lacked the deep gratitude that comes from knowing you've been spared.

The men and women who filled the auditorium had colorful pasts and incredibly hopeful futures. Some were coming back to the faith of their younger days, and some were meeting the Lord for the first time. Either way, all I could sense was an air of extreme gratefulness. The people we came to know were so delighted with their newfound freedom in the Lord because they were so painfully aware of the emptiness of their old ways.

This gratefulness shook up our tired faith and challenged us to find delight in the Lord as well. Our friends understood deeply what they had been freed from. They taught me a lot about how the freedom of Christ works itself out in our past, our present, and our future so we don't have to be shame-stuck.

Let me show you what I mean.

We Were Made in His Image and Reconciled in Christ

Just like Eve, we were made as good and lovely reflections of God Himself. We were made to look just like our Father, a spitting image. But because Eve bought into a massive lie that she ought to have all the knowledge of God, the world has not continued as God created it. We were very much created in God's image, but we also share the lineage of the first mother, Eve. We share in Eve's sinfulness in the same way I have my mom's blue-green eyes. We were born into it, and it is fully in us.

When we live wildly, we are walking in who God made us to be: bold, beautiful, and reflecting Him. But the reality is that we live in a broken world marred by sin. We are locked down by so many things. Sin, shame, fear, feeling overwhelmed—these all mark our daily lives. The thing about freedom is that you can stop trying so hard because you can rest in what Jesus has already done for you.

At the moment when Jesus died and time split in two, we were set free from a lifetime of sin and shame and invited to live in eternal communion with our Father. We're also given access to the Holy Spirit, who lives in us to guide us, comfort us, and make us more and more like our Father and desire less and less of the sin that used to mark our lives.

In a sense, we were born from our own mother with the sinful nature of humanity's first mother, Eve. But when we were reborn as a new creation in Christ, we took on His lineage and His right-eousness. This supernatural rebirth is one of the most mysterious truths of all time. In the same way that Jesus' death divided time, our choosing life in Him draws a mark straight through our lifetimes. There is *before* Christ, when self, sin, and shame were allowed to keep us down, and then *after* Christ, when we are free to be made more and more like Him.

When we are reborn in Christ, we are reconciled to God and re-created as women who are set free. We aren't tied to the selves of our past, and we aren't enslaved by the tendencies that have always plagued us. We have the Holy Spirit in our lives, who daily nudges and reminds us that the cord has already been cut. We're no longer tied to Eve's sin, but instead we're set free through Christ.

We Are Forgiven for Our Past

It can be hard to believe there is really a dividing line between the old us and the new us. But when Christ laid down His life for you, He also laid down an undeniable division at the moment you believed in Him and accepted His invitation of life. It's like a giant banner of love. Everything before that moment is utterly forgiven. The slate is wiped clean. There is no filing cabinet of your rights and wrongs.

It's one thing to believe that God doesn't hold you to the just punishment of your sin. But sometimes we want to hold ourselves accountable to our past that's already been forgiven. We want to replay the wrongs we've done and hold on to our old selves like an old blanket. Some of us have grown so comfortable with shame that we'd be uncomfortable to have the blanket pulled away. It would be like opening the blinds on a bright morning—the sun outside is good, but it makes us uncomfortable when we've been cocooned in darkness.

When I was a new believer, two women in my life led a bunch of my teenage girlfriends and me through a book called *The Green*

Letters. It felt like an ancient text to me, having been written by a man named Miles Stanford, who was born in 1914. Stanford had a rich ministry of correspondence in which he discipled other people through letter writing. His letters were compiled, edited, and published by Zondervan.

My friends and I adored *The Green Letters.* I still have my copy, which is completely beat-up, highlighted, and well-loved. It was heady and complicated writing, but somehow it simplified the most profound spiritual truths. I remember spending weeks trying to understand the idea of putting off our old self (Romans 6:6) and clothing ourselves instead in the righteousness of Jesus (Romans 13:14). It still trips people up today.

Stanford communicated it this way: "By faith in the positional fact that our Father has placed us in His Son, we abide in Him, we acknowledge our place in Him. By faith, we stand in the position He has already given us."[8]

A young woman I know had lived a hard life. She fell headlong into the bondage of disordered eating and drug abuse. She was living to forget some massive wrongs that had been committed against her. Everything she did was in the hope of overcoming the darkness she felt in her heart. Nothing worked, however, and her tactics became more and more desperate. She ended up overdosing, and at her lowest, she met Jesus. She feels He pulled her out of a miry pit of her own creation—the consequences of looking for healing in a way that would only bring bondage. She has been following Jesus for many years now and positively glows with her adoration for Him. She really believes that her old self died that day she overdosed and that she now lives in Christ alone.

We are re-created and free because we have died to ourselves and live in Christ. When we accept the beautiful gift of salvation, we are essentially taking off our own flesh and putting on the goodness of Christ.

We Are Forgiven for Our Present

There is a weird phenomenon I've noticed in the lives of Christians I know. At the beginning of our Christian walk, we're overcome with the newness and goodness of our salvation in Jesus. It's all bright and hopeful and magical. We've been forgiven for much, and we know it because it's fresh.

But after a while, the newness dulls, and we move into the patterns and rhythms of life as a Christian. It's then that people feel compelled to measure up and live by the rules of Christian culture. We can be tempted to become expert Pharisees, looking great and up to snuff on the outside, but forgetting that our inner lives need tending and renewing even still.

I knew it was good news to be forgiven of all the junk I'd done before I met Christ. But I was still human here on earth, and I was still prone to sin. It felt exhausting and shame-inducing to try to live up to a perfect standard I didn't have power on my own to achieve. It was truly good news to realize that I was forgiven in real time in every moment. If I could recognize my sin, repent, look to the Lord, and resist shame, I could take hold of the gospel and apply that good news to my everyday life. It was only by God's power that I was being sanctified anyway, not by my own goodness or hard work.

Preach the gospel to yourself every day. Come alive again in the freedom you found when you first received the good news. When you root out darkness in your heart, take it before the Lord and feel Him wash you clean again in that very moment. The good news is just as good for you today as it was the day you first believed. God didn't suddenly expect you to pull yourself up by your bootstraps and get it done yourself. You don't hold the power to save yourself or to make yourself good, and God didn't start expecting that of you just because you met Jesus.

As humans, we keep going back to holding ourselves up and making ourselves good. It is totally counterintuitive to release the power, but that's essentially what you do when you become a believer. You give up your perceived power to save yourself; you submit to the Lord and hand over your power to Him.

We Are Held in Our Future

When we cede power to the Lord, we put our care into really good hands. His hands created the universe. With just one word, He spoke things into being. We come alive in the knowledge that we are not, in fact, the ones who keep the world spinning.

I'm most paralyzed when I get it stuck in my head that it's my job to keep this whole thing going. When I feel in charge of my family's well-being, when I desire ultimate control over my health and comfort, when I feel like things won't get done unless I do them myself—those are big-time warning bells for me. When those feelings start creeping in, I know I've started to buy into the lie again that my strength is needed, though His alone *is* enough.

I had a long season after I had my first two boys when I began to doubt the goodness of God. It coincided with a time that was particularly beautiful and particularly challenging. All of a sudden, I had these two dear boys, and I wanted nothing more than to protect them with everything I had. The problem was, I also became intimately aware that my ability to protect them fell woefully short in the grand scheme of life.

Instead of realizing this was a good thing and that God is the ultimate caregiver, I bought into the lie that I had to try to keep it all together. This is ultimately a lie of pride, whispering that we're better off going it alone.

What followed was two years of intense anxiety that created a whole host of health problems. My mind was betraying my body, and my body was tricking my mind. It was a vicious cycle that constantly had me in a state of hypervigilance, always waiting for the other shoe to drop. It wasn't until my third son, Asher, was unexpectedly born very ill that I was forced to reckon with the fact that I had zero control over their lives.

Asher's name means "blessed, fortunate, and full of abundant life." Full and whole, bone of my bone, flesh of my flesh. And he was born as sick as could be. Imagine that happening.

I didn't. I knew his labor would likely be fast and furious, like those of his two brothers before him. I was fairly certain he'd have a head full of hair, as the other two had. I was certain his daddy would adore him from the first moment. I certainly didn't imagine things wouldn't go smoothly, that we wouldn't be just as blessed and fortunate as we were with our first boys.

Really, though, we *were* blessed. Of course we were blessed. It is impossible not to be blessed when tiny feet and a baby's soft skin are involved. But oh, we did not *feel* fortunate.

Asher was sick. He was so sick. His tiny body couldn't handle the immense infection that had invaded for some reason—we still don't know the cause. The doctor's words—"septic shock" and "body functions shutting down"—still echo in my ears. I still feel the sting of the hot sobs. I still remember wanting to get as close to the floor as possible, feeling like the world was spinning and wasn't to be trusted. Things were not right. This baby, my baby—he should be well.

Not even twelve hours after he was born, seemingly perfectly healthy, he was paralyzed and on a ventilator, rushed by ambulance to a specialized hospital. I went toe-to-toe with my desire to control my life when the neonatal doctor described Asher's life-threatening condition. My first thought was, *People die on* Grey's Anatomy *from septic shock*. My second was to ask the neonatologist if Asher was going to be OK.

The doctor looked at me solemnly and answered that it was always their hope that babies would pull out of this. However, newborns have a very difficult time localizing infection, and once it hits their bloodstream, like Asher's had, it was hard to predict the outcome. His organs had already started to fail, and it was anyone's best guess how he'd fare. Some babies just don't make it.

I came face-to-face with my lack of control in this life. I now know what it feels like to sorrowfully "rend your garments," as it says in the Bible. I understand now why someone would be overcome by the urge to tear their clothes off. I know your body can viscerally and innately respond; I know what it feels like to be so in your body and so out of your body at the same time.

Here's the thing. I didn't *really* believe I wasn't in control until I looked death in the eye and had to place my newborn son in the Lord's care. It wasn't a magical moment of transformation; in fact, those were some of the darkest days of my life. But in that moment, as I lay flat on the cold hospital floor, I knew for a fact that I wasn't in control anymore. And like anything in life, admitting it is the first step to accepting it.

God held my son in His hands. He healed Asher, and we eventually took him home to meet his brothers. Really, He's still holding Asher. He's holding you, and He's holding me. He cares for us much more than lilies or sparrows, yet He completely sustains *them*. They don't strive for the sun; they just open their faces toward the light and soak it in. They don't call for more rain; they just drink it up as it comes down.

We can really live with no fear of the future because we are held tightly in His hands, loved dearly and accepted fully as His daughters. But we must believe He is good in order to quietly lie down in His provision.

We Are Fully Known and Fully Loved

God longs for us to experience His freedom for good reason—because it is His gift to those He knows and loves. And it is a gift He has obtained through great personal cost.

Psalm 139 is an incredibly intimate section of the Bible that speaks of God's great love and care for us. In this psalm, we read beautiful poetry of God's intimate knowledge of our creation and our lives. If you've never read it, now is the perfect time. And even if you have, I'd challenge a slow rereading to refresh and encourage your belief in a God who knows you and loves you. Sometimes it can be near impossible to fathom that we have a God who knows our thoughts before we think them and our words before we say them—and loves us still the same.

> You have searched me, LORD,
>> and you know me.
> You know when I sit and when I rise;
>> you perceive my thoughts from afar.
> You discern my going out and my lying down;
>> you are familiar with all my ways.
> Before a word is on my tongue
>> you, LORD, know it completely.
> You hem me in behind and before,
>> and you lay your hand upon me.
> Such knowledge is too wonderful for me,
>> too lofty for me to attain.
> Where can I go from your Spirit?
>> Where can I flee from your presence?
> If I go up to the heavens, you are there;
>> if I make my bed in the depths, you are there.

If I rise on the wings of the dawn,
>if I settle on the far side of the sea,
even there your hand will guide me,
>your right hand will hold me fast.
If I say, "Surely the darkness will hide me
>and the light become night around me,"
even the darkness will not be dark to you;
>the night will shine like the day,
>for darkness is as light to you.
For you created my inmost being;
>you knit me together in my mother's womb.
I praise you because I am fearfully and wonderfully made;
>your works are wonderful,
>I know that full well.
My frame was not hidden from you
>when I was made in the secret place,
>when I was woven together in the depths of the earth.
Your eyes saw my unformed body;
>all the days ordained for me were written in your book
>before one of them came to be.

Psalm 139:1–16

It's incredible to learn that He stitched us together, tucked away in our mother's belly. We know we cannot hide from Him, because He'll find us in the dark. We cannot run away from Him, because He'll seek us even from across the ocean.

To be fully known and fully loved gives us immense and crazy freedom to be the woman God made us to be, to respond to the Holy Spirit without fear, and to love without reservation. He has equipped us fully with His power and truth.

Being fully known on a human plane helps us understand being fully known on a heavenly plane. It puts flesh on an abstract idea.

My first real taste of the freedom that comes from being totally seen and totally accepted came when I was sixteen and had just started dating my husband-to-be.

Mike and I had met about a month before, and like teenagers do, we'd become inseparable fairly quickly. We wanted to spend all of our minutes together, but we went to different schools and therefore had totally different groups of pals. We also didn't want to be those people who met someone and then disappeared off the face of the earth, so we tried to still have regular time apart with our respective groups of friends.

One night, Mike had a guys' night with his friends from school, which meant I had to find something to do to occupy my evening. I ended up hanging out with a group of my friends from youth group, and I was on the receiving end of a lot of attention from a boy I'd had a crush on in years past.

To make a long story short, this boy and I shared what was really a very innocent kiss, but it wasn't innocent in the context of my new relationship with Mike. I knew it would hurt Mike, and I immediately felt a crazy amount of shame and regret. I wanted to hide the truth, but I was struck by the honesty we had together because we'd started our relationship with Christ. I'd never met anyone like Mike, and I knew I had to tell him what happened, even if it meant ruining everything we could have had.

To make matters worse, I came home to an email from Mike letting me know that while he'd had a great night, he'd really wished I had been there. I felt shame all the way to my bones, and my desire to avoid confrontation was strong. I wanted to just walk away from the budding potential of our relationship and burn the bridge we'd barely begun to cross.

That's what my family always did, and avoiding and leaving was what was most comfortable for me. But I felt a whisper from the Holy Spirit to stay and trust Him to give me the strength and the words.

The next night, Mike and I were going to get together with his friends to watch some college basketball. Being from Indiana, I know basketball is serious business, and I didn't want to spoil Mike's plans with bad news at the beginning of the night. So we went to dinner with his parents to start the evening, and I was so nervous because of this secret that I spilled lemonade down the front of my shirt. The rest of the evening didn't go any better.

I refused to hold Mike's hand or get too near him because I was certain he'd be furious when he heard the truth. He'd be angry that I'd still let him get close. Mike sensed that something was up and pressed me for answers on the car ride home. I knew I had to tell him, but I also wanted to wait just a few more minutes until he was closer to my house. I was sure he'd kick me out of the car right on the side of the road.

But instead, when I told him the hard truth, he drove silently in the opposite direction of my childhood home. He pulled up to a park with a swing set, opened my door, and took my hand. He sat me down on a swing and kneeled in front of me. He went on to tell me how hurt he was, how this wasn't what he would have hoped for, but that he had already decided he was in this relationship. He wasn't scared off by immaturity on my part.

Mike told me in no uncertain terms that the only way this young relationship was going to work was if I decided it was worth not walking away from. He told me he forgave me, but he needed to hear that I was in this as much as he was. He wanted to have my buy-in and to know I had skin in the game.

In that moment, I felt exposed like never before. My offense was laid out in front of me for both of us to see clearly. But even when the ugliest part of me was known, I was accepted and forgiven. That night still stands out as the most heavenly moment of human grace I've ever experienced, the kind that comes from being known and yet still chosen.

That grace allowed me the freedom to grow into our relationship and ultimately, over the years, into myself. Mike's selfless grace granted me the room to discover more of Christ and more of myself. He has, to this day, never brought up that offense from almost fifteen years ago. He has never held it over my head or used the truth as a weapon. That forgiveness was my first taste of the freedom that comes from real love.

God offers this freedom to us a millionfold. He loves us as far as the sea is wide and all the way up to the stars. He sees us fully, down to the most intimate depths, and still chooses to spend all of eternity with us, as long as we decide we're in it. He asks us to lay it all out in front of Him because He knows the freedom that comes when you have skin in the game and you're fully known.

We Are Fully Seen and Fully Chosen

When we are seen and still chosen, there is no room for shame. Shame only flourishes in the dark, and there is no darkness in the Lord. When we rightly understand our position as re-created and free, we can live out our freedom with confidence. You are truly free. Your freedom was won on the cross and secured by your Father in your Christian life. It is not something you have to try to do; it is something that is simply true of you. You are seen, you are chosen, and you are free.

Let's take hold of that truth, just like any other truth in the Bible. If it's hard for you to believe, ask God to help you in your unbelief. Ask Him to show you the depths of yourself so you can finally believe that if you're in Christ, He's made you new and He sees Jesus when He looks at you. You don't have to do more or try harder, because you can't manufacture this kind of freedom on your own. This is a soul-shifting, bone-deep kind of freedom that changes your life forever.

If you've had a moment like this, like my friend had when he overdosed or like I had when my sin was exposed to Mike, will you take some time to write it down? Will you make that moment a little Ebenezer from 1 Samuel 7:12, a monument of remembrance? Describe what the shame and pain felt like, and then spend some time writing down your thoughts about how you *knew* that Jesus had already done the work to set you free. To me, this feels like an important moment in your spiritual history, one to look back on and celebrate or recall when you struggle with doubts. The moment you first understand rescue, mercy, and grace frees you up for a lifetime of living in freedom.

PRAYER

Father, show us. Show us how free we are. Show us what that looks like. Will you reveal to us why freedom is important to you? Why you so long for us to believe we have it? Will you show us why you broke the chains of bondage in our lives? Will you show us your lavish love?

God, sometimes it's hard to really believe it. Will you help us overcome our unbelief? Will you offer some kind and tangible reminders of your love for us and how your work on the cross changed everything?

We want to believe that everything was different when we accepted your Son's sacrifice. We want to believe that the gospel changes us every day. Will you make that shine for us, Lord? Please show each of us in the ways that we understand, God.

JESS'S RESPONSE

"We are forgiven for our present." Man, am I glad Hayley wrote that! I think it's so interesting that as believers we're so comfortable with receiving grace for our past (even a few days past!), but the idea of walking around constantly needing God and His grace makes us so itchy. I personally think it's really dicey when believers work really hard to defend their present character, as if they're now—in the moment—immune to sin. I'm a sinner saved by grace. I'm redeemed, and God is working in me every minute. I'm living in the victory of the cross, but I'm still very much also living in this world where the weight of sin hangs on me and I do things I don't want to do and don't do the things my redeemed heart very much wants to do.

Let's not be shocked by our own sin—or anyone else's. Let's be shocked and amazed and *blessed* by the great love and redemption of our Father, who forgives our past, our present, and our future sins.

Your Invitation
Back to the Wild

In the spring of 2011, I was in the thick of it. Our family lived in a tiny two-bedroom house out in the middle of nowhere in a city we vowed never to live in again. Nick and I lovingly called the house "the fishing shack" because it just didn't quite seem like a normal home for many reasons. It had superhard cement floors with just a thin layer of indoor/outdoor carpeting to cushion our feet. All of our pieces of furniture were hand-me-downs and mismatched. The walls were covered in the darkest and dreariest wood paneling—my arch nemesis.

During that season, Nick and I shared a car, and he worked a dull and dreary job he lovingly tolerated for the sake of our family. He'd already received the call to church planting, straight from the Lord, but had put off the actual action steps to build a church due to some family issues. The place where he worked, in a monotonous and tiny cubicle, was about thirty minutes away from the fishing shack. Whenever I wanted to go anywhere with our three kids for any length of time during the day, I'd have to drive him (with the kids) thirty minutes there and back in the morning and once again in the afternoon. Because of this, the kids and I stayed home a lot. They were four, three, and two and so fun—but such a handful.

The days were colorless and dull at best, but in all honesty—we were just so grateful. That bland life we were living was one of rescue. The pocket-sized and unappealing house had been rented to us at a massive discount to help us climb out of financial distress. The car that faithfully carried us hours and hours each week was a gift of mercy, given to us for free by a friend when we had to sell ours. The kids were at overwhelming ages, but they were there. In the months prior, we'd lost one baby to miscarriage and nearly lost our three-year-old daughter due to a debilitating problem with seizures.

And me? I was finally emotionally and mentally stable after a crippling battle with anxiety and depression. The panic attacks, suicidal thoughts, and days of feeling incapable of getting out of bed were finally fewer and further between. We weren't living our dream life, and we certainly weren't living anyone else's dream. But we were *alive* by the skin of our teeth. We were still together, still standing, and still calling on the name of the Lord.

I constantly felt insecure about our little fishing shack and tried to make it look more normal. I had a friend who was a supercreative home décor blogger. I'd occasionally go over to her house and just want to hide. Her home was creative and always shifting, as she'd receive new inspiration daily. But her yard. Oh, ladies, her yard is what really made me feel insecure. She seemed to have straight-up dominion over those plants—beautiful flowering bushes, hanging baskets, and more potted plants than I could count. At the fishing shack, we had a yard full of leaves, sand, and snakes, and one abandoned concrete planter attached to the front of the house. Nothing grandiose lived in there except dirt and my kids' leftover toys.

During that season, I had a dream that massively shifted my soul and the way I viewed life with Christ. Ultimately, God used it for my healing and restoration. But more than that, He really started to whisper wild and free to me. A wind of promise and hope and *something more* was blowing into my life while I slept.

In my dream, I found myself standing in front of that concrete planter with my amazing blogger friend positioned just beside me.

As we were looking down at the dirt, the soil started shifting and flowers began growing, right in front of our eyes. First, little green buds popped up, and then longer stalks began to appear. To our amazement, small sprouts turned into bursts of color, and those colors unfurled into huge blooms. The flowers kept growing, spilling out of the planter, over our feet, and into the wide-open yard. I stood there, mouth agape, pointing and showing my friend, and in that moment, I heard Father say, "See? Things aren't supposed to grow here, but they will."

I woke up with one real truth stuck in my head and in my heart: Our circumstances and our surroundings do not dictate how wild God can be. The wild and free nature of God does not bat an eyelash at the state we're in, because He is not bound by the conventional, the typical, or any rules. Our lives can look shattered and bland, broken and poor—and He can bring life and salvation and color, no matter what. Jesus did not die on the cross only for the people with the pretty houses, and the sweet wind of the Holy Spirit does not flow only through tidy lives. I'm not a gal who dreams often or prophetically, and I rarely even remember my dreams, but most days I feel like I still live inside of what I saw that night. And since then, my heart has believed that flowers can bloom on His command in dry and deserted places, flowing past our feet and spilling into the world.

My circumstances didn't change overnight. I didn't move out of the fishing shack for almost another year. But the dream opened my eyes, and continues to open them, to see past my initial physical perceptions of who I am and how life is going for me. When my bank account is low, I'm reminded that God's bounty is not bound by anything. When my spirit feels heavy and despair feels near, I'm reminded that the wild Spirit of God that raised Christ from the dead still lives in me and has dominion over any darkness. None of this means our days will never be hard, dusty, or occasionally dry—it just means when we have hearts that walk wild with God, we're using a different measuring stick of our circumstances.

I wish I could step back into that dream and take every single one of you with me. I wish we could stand together and let the blooms tickle our ankles because they're growing so fast and strong. If we could, I'd probably make you awkwardly hold my hand, and I'd tell you this: Not only is God bigger and wilder than your circumstances, and not only can He do whatever He wants in your life, but you are already wild. You don't have to put it on or build it up. If Christ is in you, the wild nature of God is ready for you to access and practice and live out. You, sister-friend, are already wild. This means, simply put, that you don't live subject to any constraints or categories. You can defy expectation and throw off any and all assumptions, because that is the nature of the God who lives in you.

The number one question Hayley and I get when we start talking about wild and free is this: "What does it look like?" Thankfully, we honestly have an abundance of truth and examples from God's Word, but it is imperative not to read them as a to-do list. Anytime we encounter human attributes or characteristics in the Word or in Christian writings, we are tempted to measure ourselves against it. *Am I that? Am I close to that? What would I need to do to be that?* But the very act of measuring ourselves against attributes of wild is counterproductive, because it cages us again inside another expectation. Living as a wild daughter of the King is not a level to achieve; it's a freedom we all currently possess. If Christ is in you, you have access to wild and free living *right now*. You're as holy as you'll ever be, as wild as you'll ever be, as free as you'll ever be, and as loved by God as you'll ever be.

As time goes on, the wild muscle will absolutely grow, and its expression can become stronger and stronger. The more you practice your liberty from defensive living, the quicker you'll find your reaction time to let your outsides match your liberated insides. But it's so important not to read the description of wild as a to-do list, a definitive list, or a benchmark to obtain. Your God is bigger than that; you are *already* wild; and these are just some characteristics that you already possess in Christ and that the Holy Spirit will continue to refine.

I believe this especially strongly for myself, as I'm writing this book on wild and free and know I'm nowhere near living out the fullness of all of these descriptions. The ability to spend minutes, hours, and whole days being trapped by my culture or my fears is so near to me, but we keep pressing on and practicing wild for the sake of God's glory and our good.

Without further ado, here is an incomplete and abridged list of what wild can look like.

Here She Is—the Wild Woman Herself

Wild women are secure in their identity because their eyes are on the Lord. They aren't comfortable with who they are because they've achieved some level of goodness or righteousness. They aren't comfortable with who they are because they have enough money or beauty. Wild women live at ease with all their weaknesses and strengths, sin and spiritual gifts, because they are inextricably rooted in a God who covers and uses it all. They know that the less they think about themselves, the more they're thinking about Him, and that's a good thing. As Ephesians 1:18 declares, the eyes of their heart have been enlightened, and they've seen the hope that they're called to and the riches of the glorious inheritance they have as God's children, and how incomparably great His power is for them. A wild woman doesn't have time or space to feel insecure, because her thoughts and affections are for Him and for how immeasurably great He is.

A wild woman is soft to her need for the gospel and open to correction from God and others. In the world's view of wild, one might run far in her own strength and power and be unwilling to feel broken, to be seen as weak, or to hear truth spoken to her. In our beautiful and redeemed view of wild, we know that since we are safe and secure as daughters, we have no need to hide our humanity. The very gospel we love and preach, we need. Wild women know they're still sinners saved by grace, being transformed daily by the power of the Holy Spirit. But they're sinners. They will hurt others and be hurt; they will need to forgive and ask for forgiveness. Wild women don't hide from God or humans when they screw up; they hold their hands open and walk in humility. A wild woman can hear correction and know that people aren't telling her there's something fundamentally wrong with her, because she's covered in the blood of Jesus. She lives and celebrates the glorious truth of 2 Corinthians 12:9—she knows His power is made perfect in her weaknesses, and she cannot take anything away from His power by letting herself be weak.

I often encourage women to do this when they need a gospel refresher: Remember that you cannot be found out. No one can expose you. When we come to Jesus and begin a relationship with Him, we come humbled and stay humbled. We need Him the first day to redeem us, and we'll need Him the last day of our lives as well. You cannot be found out. You are found in Christ Jesus.

A wild woman doesn't toil; she works from approval, not for approval. You won't hear a woman who walks wild with the Lord bemoaning that she doesn't know how God will use her particular gifts or calling in His kingdom. She believes Psalm 16:6 and recognizes that her place is found right where God has put her and that He's drawn pleasant boundary lines for her. She knows her calling is to live as part of the royal nation and holy priesthood that is meant to declare God's praises to those who've not yet seen the marvelous light. But she also knows in her very core that *she* is God's workmanship, and He doesn't need her to produce anything. She doesn't need to earn her spot at the table or do a certain amount of deeds to matter in His kingdom. The work of her hands right where she is, combined with the Spirit in her soul, produces beautiful and sweet fruit.

A wild woman is able to hear the cry of a hurting world. It might be the neighbor next door or the village five thousand miles away—she doesn't need to pretend like it's not happening and keep going on with her own life. Because the Holy Spirit is living and active in her, He has tuned her heart to see injustice and hear lamentation and *do* something about it. She keeps God on the throne as the ultimate healer and fixer of all things, so she is able to care for people without trying to carry their burdens for them.

A wild woman speaks the native language of her Father—life. Because her Father used phrases during creation like "let there be" and "this is good," she knows her tongue is always at home speaking life. She speaks life and truth over herself, not bashing who He's made her to be and not beating anyone else to the punch to point out her faults. A woman who is wild for God knows the eternal power in her words and uses them carefully and passionately with those around her. She greets others with excitement, and she is much more of a "there you are!" person than a "here I am!" kind of girl. She is encouraging, admonishing, and truthful, and she isn't scared of using her words to speak correction because she knows that doing so occasionally brings life as well. You won't hear her talking about the things she can't do, and she'll never speak the phrase "shame on you" to anyone, because she wants wild freedom for everyone else as much as she wants it for herself.

A wild woman doesn't see life from a place of lack. You can call her an optimist or talk about how she always sees the glass half full, but she knows the alternative is not giving God room to move and not counting the fruit of what He's doing. She sees herself not as a pile of faults and mistakes but as a tapestry of grace and a weaving of God's great mercy. She doesn't see all your past sins or the ability you have to wound her; she sees you covered in the blood of Jesus, with a glorious cloud of witnesses cheering you on. When a wild woman is confronted with a problem, she doesn't immediately lament over how bad it is, because she knows God is working all things for her good—so there is most likely some blessing or benefit for her that she cannot see. She doesn't talk about what she can't afford or how busy she is, because Psalm 50:10 tells her that her Dad owns the cattle on a thousand hills and is the One who invented time, so ultimately she *will* have all she needs.

A wild woman runs hard and fast, without baggage. She knows this life is not a sprint or a short race but a long and grace-filled marathon. She also knows it's not her strength but the Lord's that pushes her forward. A wild woman, once oriented in the direction of God's kingdom, doesn't want to stop to care too much about herself, though she will stop to take care of herself. This means she's not scared to rest but does have an aversion to being spiritually idle for the sake of indulgence. She sees her life as long but her days as numbered, and she just wants to go as far as He'll go with her, as far as He'll carry her. She is not easily offended or dissuaded or confused, because her eyes are on her one and only prize—being one with Christ alone.

If I could sit with you right now, I'd make you some coffee or tea and get uncomfortably close enough to know you were really listening. I have something incredibly essential you need to know about this wild woman, and you cannot miss it—or else you miss everything.

You are her.

You are the wildest woman of God you know. If you've been reborn in Christ, accepting His love and grace for yourself personally, then I don't care what you've done or how trapped you feel or how out of control you've spun. You are a mighty daughter of God, and *you are wild*. It may take time to walk with Him, to learn His rhythms, to watch as He removes the shackles you've been carrying around—but He can do it effortlessly.

Jesus Christ died on the cross so you wouldn't live inside a small and scared box. He rose from the dead and defeated sin so your only picture of freedom didn't need to be living angrily, defensively, and fighting to be heard. You're already free. You're already wild. That woman is you.

Theoretically and theologically, you *are* that wild woman, but I know you might not always feel like it. Goodness, as I type these words, I don't really feel like it. So how do we get to a place of living out our identity every day of our lives? How do we shake off the cages and the expectations and the rhythms of operating and truly wake up? First, let's reapply the truth that our circumstances and surroundings never dictate what God can do or how wild we can be. Our feet are planted firmly in the flowers that should never have grown here. Then let's move forward.

Let's Get Weird

When I get the opportunity to speak to women about Jesus, I like to invite them to respond however they need to. Me? In church or at conferences, I cannot physically sit still to save my life. I will twirl my hair contemplatively; I'll doodle on every square inch of my Bible and notebook as I take notes; or you might find me crying or swaying. And during worship, watch out! My arm might hit you, or my haphazardly dancing/stomping feet might come down on your pinky toe. I know some women like to sit and listen attentively and calmly, and that is 100 percent freedom for them, but I have to get a little weird. I often tell my husband that no part of serving in our church plant is harder for me than sitting on the front row so I can make eye contact while he preaches. On the front row, I feel like I must be still and quiet. And I am *not* still or quiet.

So on the occasions when I'm speaking, I genuinely feel much more comfortable if whoever is listening exercises their freedom to get weird as well. They can talk back to me from the crowd or get on the floor and lie down. If they need to leave in the middle to pray with a friend, all the better. A loud sob here and there encourages me that we're headed somewhere, and a shouted "Amen!" is my jam. Just please, God, don't let me have to look at hundreds of women who are staring straight back at me, expressionless, probably thinking how messy my hair is.

And here's my encouragement to you. If you're going to live as wild as you already are, you're going to have to get weird. Think about it: God bringing light out of darkness? Walking on water? Raising Jesus from the dead? God, in His utter wildness, defies all the laws of the natural order. It's wild; it's weird—and we want to live that kind of wild freedom. We are called to follow suit. You're going to have to ask that girl if you can pray for her, the one you absolutely cannot get off your heart. You're going to have to occasionally give up on having a sofa with perfectly straightened pillows so you can lie down and cuddle with your kids and speak some life over them.

To be truly wild, you may have to stay quiet when everyone else is gossiping or tearing someone down. What's more, you may have to get weird and loud and speak some truth when you know it's time for injustice to stop. You may be the only one taking time to rest or pause because God said so, or you may be the only one working and pushing when no one else seems to care. Your love and grace and forgiveness may seem out of place in the lives around you, and the way you stand confident in your identity will be countercultural, no matter your age.

My sister's friend Mandie Joy may seem weird to the world because she has two adopted daughters, four foster kids, and no husband—but to me she is wildly obedient to God's call on her life. It was weird when my friend Brittany moved away from all that was safe and comfortable and expected of her to live with us in South Carolina and start a church with only six people. But I believe God's gotten some wild glory out of that decision. Some may have called it weird when my precious friend Rachael married a man who already had two sons, but God was wild in her heart and life, and today she's the best mom and stepmom I know. It was certainly weird when Lindsay and I became close, intimate friends and confidantes, though our businesses should've been each other's biggest competitors. But we trusted our wild God, and He has brought wild fruit to both businesses like only He can.

You will be weird occasionally, but you will be wild. You may be seen as strange or different, but you will be seen and loved fully by God. If we're still believing that God can bring more abundance to our lives than we could ask or imagine, and we're accepting of the fact that our freedom will be mistaken for strange, let's get off our sweet and tidy ornamental princess thrones and take our place in the kingdom of God. We have a solidified identity full of gifts we're ready to use, and we're not ashamed of looking a little crazy. We're ready to walk wildly.

Find Your Gateway

The Christmas before I had the "beautiful flower" dream, I received a simple and life-changing gift from my mama. My mom is the queen gift giver. She doesn't stop by my house on a random

Tuesday without having a little goody bag, so you can imagine how much she loves to bless during the holidays. She'd bought my sisters and me each a small piece of jewelry, and when I opened mine, I was immediately a little dismayed. She must have mixed them up; this couldn't have been for me. It was a *huge*, honking ring with a ginormous red flower on it. I loved it! But I knew it was probably for my older sister, who's much more stylish and is always wearing some fun and trendy outfit. As I got ready to make the trade, the look on my mom's face said she hadn't made a mistake. My heart processed this news quickly, and my eyes caught up sooner than my brain did. I burst into big, sloppy tears and kept saying, "This is for *me*? You meant this ring for me?" It was mind-boggling that in the midst of my vanilla, bland, lifeless season of surviving and not thriving, she saw me as spicy and bold enough to carry that ring off.

Obviously, I didn't take it off for a month. And when you're wearing a ring like that, you can't just wear dirty yoga pants and sweatshirts. So I had to dig out some cute clothes from the back of my closet, and I even hit up the thrift store to see if I could find something cheap and seemingly stylish. Once I was actually getting dressed again *and* had on my supercute ring, I noticed my nails looked kinda busted. With that big ole funky ring, I needed some funky nail polish, so I hightailed it to Target and bought a bottle of the darkest navy blue I could find and splashed it right on my fingers.

You can see where this is going. Ring. Clothes. Nails. Up until that point in my life, I'd pretty much been a ChapStick-only or lip gloss kind of gal. Who was I to put on a bold red lipstick? I couldn't pull that off. But—my mom had bought me this big, swanky ring. If she thought I could wear that ring and not look like a weirdo, maybe I *was* the kind of girl who could wear bold lipstick. I marched myself right back to Target about two days after

I bought the nail polish and purchased the strongest, punchiest red lipstick I could find. And you guys? It's been five years, but I haven't really ever taken it off. The shade might change, and I'll wear any brand I can get my hands on, but I know I'm the kind of girl who can wear red lipstick. That day, my own wild mama handed me a massive gift of confidence more than she handed me a ring. She called me up to wild living with her.

But here's the thing. Someone tells me at least once a week, "I wish I could wear red lipstick," and at least once a week I want to sit a woman down and walk her through my story. I want to tell her how my life was bland and vanilla and fearful and small. I want to tell her how I burst into tears when I opened the box with that ring in it because I didn't think I was worthy of it. And then I want to very lovingly smear the boldest and brightest shade of red I can find all over her lips, show her herself in the mirror, and prove to her that *she can be wild too.*

Being wild in the Lord isn't about wearing red lipstick, but the principles are really the same. You may see something in another woman that screams freedom or life or God on the move, and you decide it's not for you. Maybe you think you've messed up too much, or maybe you're convinced you're not a leader. Maybe you're scared you'll cause a ruckus, or maybe you've tried before and felt judged. I'm not sure what injuries of this world have gotten you to a place where you feel like you are not wild and you are not free, but I am positive that Christ our King is stronger than they are. I can promise you that in Him you are already wilder and freer than you could ever imagine. I believe you're meant to lead other women in it. I think you should try again. And I totally think you can pull off red lipstick.

You just need to find your gateway. For me, the big ring was a slippery slope to getting dressed and feeling funky, and I believe there are little gateways all over our lives that help us start tumbling toward the path to wild freedom as well. On the flip side, when women struggle with feeling small and scared, limited and held back, that gate stays shut. But there's a whole new world of wild and free that God is calling us to. We just need to kick the gate open and stop telling ourselves the lie that we're not allowed beyond it. May the walking wild begin.

Here are a few gates to consider walking through:

Read God's Word. Before you cross this one off the list, I want to talk about *how* we're reading God's Word. I think reading God's Word in community is an amazing tool, but I find so many women are reluctant to get weird and wild in their own homes by themselves. Find your Bible, head to 1 Peter 2:9 to start, and, in a quiet moment, walk around your living room reading it aloud. Read it two or three times, and say it with conviction. The next time your kids or your roommates are arguing, start reading some psalms aloud in the midst of them, or post on the bathroom mirror some Scripture verses you're claiming. Dig into God's Word. Study the stuff that scares you. Look up the Hebrew and Greek online to enhance your understanding. The Bible isn't an ancient artifact; it's an alive and active *weapon* to defeat the enemy of your God. Use it like one. I give you permission.

Pray for healing. Get a friend or start alone and identify something broken that you'd really love to see the Lord fix. It could be a broken relationship or a friend's terminal illness. Allow yourself to feel the fear of "what if He doesn't do what we're asking," and pray anyhow. Confess to Him that you're scared He isn't going to really do it. You don't have to come to Him having it all together or all figured out. Then, in the name of Jesus, ask Him to revive it and fix it. Keep doing it over and over. Put it in His hands again and again. When He brings healing, give Him all the glory and praise you can muster. If His perfect will doesn't include the result you hoped for, you will have spent all of that time in His lap talking to

Him, and I believe you will feel closer for it. Tell Him you wished it had gone your way—He's big enough to take that. Then tell Him you want to trust Him, even though you're frustrated.

Forgive someone. Stop listing the reasons you can't, and just try. Ask God to help you try. You don't have to walk back into the exact same relationship with them, but you can stop holding the sin over them, whether or not they know it. Believe that the grace of God that covers you is big enough to cover them too. Forgive yourself. If God isn't holding on to your sin, why are you? Sit at the foot of the cross and let your Father love you.

Here are a number of other things that may break through the gateway into living wild: take a walk, take a day off, watch the sunrise and thank God for it, serve someone who doesn't deserve it, paint a little (don't say you're not creative—the God who created the universe lives in you!), put on some loud worship music and dance, go on a prayer walk with friends, ask for prayer at church, write a psalm, bless someone who doesn't expect it, wear a big ring, and, of course, put on some red lipstick.

Destroy the Box

There's one last thing to do to really solidify walking as wildly as possible, and it's an ongoing project. We have to *keep taking God out of His box*—over and over again. The good news is that God is bigger than the shell or the mold or the expectations we have of Him. The bad news is that once we take Him out and see something new He wants to do, that level or action or intimacy becomes our new mold. But He is infinite. He is always moving, always shifting, always growing us, and always bigger than we can imagine.

As wild women, we've now accepted that God can do whatever He wants. No matter how busted, bruised, small, still, or normal our lives are, we believe the wind of the Holy Spirit can blow in our circumstances and through us. We've looked at a few of the biblical principles of wild living that we know we can walk in, and we're believing that those aren't to-dos for us or attributes we need to muster up. We've accepted the fact that we may seem weird to the world or—goodness—even to current Christian culture, and we're OK with that. We're looking for the triggers, the gateways to wild living that remind us He is big and we get to run with Him.

But let's keep destroying the box we're inclined to put Him in. I think we'll find that as we break down that box, we'll start setting ourselves free from similar boxes we live in. Let's break it down, throw it out, and burn it up. As we seek to know Him better and find Him more often, let's find worship and wonder and awe. Let's keep throwing out the formulas and patterns we try to attribute to Him, since He's told us He can't be figured out or grasped in whole until eternity.

Let's remember that He is the God who grows things where they're not supposed to grow, and that our feet are covered in flowers.

PRAYER

God, thank You for being one who grows things where there is no logic. We're crazy grateful for Your wild love for us. Thank You for knowing what we need and providing for us—just so. We're grateful we can't put You into a box or a pattern. Would You help us to see that as a good and lovely thing about You, Lord? We love You!

HAYLEY'S RESPONSE

First, I need to tell you: You *can* wear red lipstick! Really, you can. I am a fellow red lipstick lover, and if you don't feel sure about it, go get a $2 tube. What do you have to lose? I wear mostly neutrals and especially gray, but I cannot help but love red lipstick! I say this to encourage you, even if you feel far from wild, that you can take this first step.

Second, how absolutely gorgeous is that fishing shack dream? That is an illustration from Jess's life that I just cannot ever forget. It helps me put flesh on the idea of God being a wild and generous giver. He isn't bound by what should grow, but He has dominion over it all. I hope for that lush and wild growth in my own life.

Unchained and Unafraid

When you know what it's like to live chained and caged, you begin to see how beautiful freedom is. At least, that's been my story.

I am the oldest daughter, born and bred to please. In my flesh, I am compliant and conscientious. I am a yes-woman because I loathe letting people down. Nothing wigs me out more than the thought of making someone else uncomfortable in my presence. My deepest shame comes from making mistakes.

There are two main problems with this kind of living. First, there is the obvious issue of pride. When your outsides look like the cultural ideal, you'll get all kinds of praise, and you'll become a slave to that praise. Your life will feel empty without it. The second is that when you're used to being bright and shiny, you become absolutely capsized when you fail. Both sides of that coin are paralyzing.

Do you remember the joy you felt when you first came to know the Lord? Do you remember how you were throwing off old chains like they were weightless? Do you remember feeling powerful because you had just learned that your Father is powerful?

I remember the months following my faith aha moment with sweet nostalgia. I was bold and excited and wanted everyone to know the reason. I felt exhilarated—like I was seeing the world with new eyes.

I met the Lord coming off a bit of a rebellious time in my

life. During my sophomore year in high school, my parents were coming out of their divorce and trying to reestablish themselves as independent adults. They had lots of nights away from home, and I was often left to my own devices. Even though I have a hardwired sense of right and wrong, this was the first time in my life that I started to walk on the wrong side of decisions—on purpose.

I was sneaking out of the house, meeting up with boys, and consuming a lot of alcohol for the sole purpose of getting really, really drunk. I was making outrageous decisions, and as I look back on it as an adult, I know I wanted someone to catch me and pay attention to me.

But I never got caught by my parents. I never got in serious trouble, and I praise God all the time that I was spared from long-term consequences of the decisions I made when I was fifteen. Instead of being caught and punished, I was found out by God and set free. He saw all of my mess and loved me all the same.

My life changed because of God's immense grace. It wasn't just that God's grace allowed me to change; God's grace *compelled* me to change. I remember the moment when I understood the foundational idea of sanctification and the growth of the Christian life. I was singing the 1990s worship song "Lord, Reign in Me" and raised my hands at the lyrics "let my life reflect the beauty of my Lord." That is the moment God reached through infinity and grasped my heart. He was holding me, and I felt free. I want to remember that initial freedom, even when I'm tempted to be led into bondage yet again. I want to live a life of real freedom. The good news is, we have the ability to live that way every single day.

What a Free Woman Looks Like

A woman who is free is unchained from her past and unafraid of her future, and because of this she can laugh at the days to come. She's got an assured confidence; she doesn't let circumstances shake her; she loves people but doesn't live to please them. She is content with what she has, never striving to conjure up something more.

She is almost inexplicably light and unencumbered. Isn't this the way we'd live if we really believed we were freed from our past, held in our present, and protected in our future?

So what does this free woman look like? We don't have to look any further than Scripture to get an idea of God's great hope for us. We look at His commands and His character to discern His best for us.

She can laugh at the days to come; she is content; she abides; and she rests.

> She is clothed with strength and dignity;
> she can laugh at the days to come.
>
> *Proverbs 31:25*

I have always had this underlying fear of the other shoe dropping. Sometimes it feels like life is just *too good*. I have almost everything I've always hoped for, prayed for. Isn't this about when God comes in and cuts down the heroine at the knees, forcing her to trust Him and obey Him even more? I started living in demented fear of God rather than a holy awe. I was conjuring up worst-case scenarios in a best-of-times situation.

Right after the birth of our second son, I began feeling a weakness and heaviness in my right leg. At first, I passed it off as a random oddity, but I became more and more obsessed as the days went on. I started med school on WebMD and began a monthlong process of hypervigilance and self-diagnosis. It didn't help that my symptoms mimicked some very real and scary maladies. I was convinced my symptoms were nefarious, and I began to imagine all the ways God would grow my faith in the suffering caused by these terrible diseases.

What I realized after going to many specialists was that God was allowing me to suffer severe anxiety rather than a life-threatening illness. When my brain latched on to an anxious thought, my body would be flushed with adrenaline. When that adrenaline stayed at high enough levels over an extended period of time, my body experienced real physical symptoms. Every symptom was eventually tied back to anxiety.

Somehow, over a period of months, I was able to learn to speak truth to my physical feelings. I started to believe the doctors over the lies in my head. And almost like magic, my symptoms began to fade.

But just a couple years later, I felt the all-too-familiar revving up of symptoms and worries. I had gone more than two years speaking truth and life to myself, but I was getting tired, and life had thrown us a few curveballs. I began to experience an onslaught of anxiety expressed as physical symptoms. Instead of being able to name the physical feelings as manifestations of my mental anxieties, I began again to believe they were tied to unfortunate, terrifying, and most of the time terminal diseases. It got to the point where I remember sitting at lunch with my husband and three boys and seeing all of them talking, but the only thoughts in my head were obsessions about my imminent demise.

Things worsened considerably, and eventually I couldn't leave the couch and could barely lift my head off the pillow. My anxiety was presenting itself like it always had, mimicking symptoms of serious illnesses. I was so weak and so terribly convinced that God was preparing to take me from this precious life I'd built.

But in His goodness, He provided a way out of that miry pit. It took a round of antidepressants and antianxiety medication, as well as months of therapy, but by the end of the summer, I began to feel the fog lifting.

I didn't trust in God's goodness because I had inadvertently bought into some terrible theology. You see, in simple terms, theology is what we believe to be true about God. Somehow I picked up the belief that God would *cause* terrible things to happen to me, and He'd do it to teach me a lesson. So in a momentary brave assertion that I believed God to be true, I went on a search for what the goodness of God really means. Now, I believe that God allows the brokenness of this diseased world to play out sometimes, leaving us with things like multiple sclerosis and cancer. *He doesn't cause these awful things, but He allows them.* That was a big shift in my mentality. If something so sad would befall me, His child, He would have holy sorrow but not be surprised and would make sure to use it for my good and for His glory. That was infinitely comforting and has allowed me to walk forward in freedom from the excruciating anxiety I lived with for many years.

Even when it's incredibly hard to understand, we get to believe that God is good and will continue being good. We get to place our trust in Him in the midst of lives that sometimes don't make sense. Ultimately, that is where most of us find this understanding of God's goodness. Most of us forget to stop and praise Him for being good when our lives are plodding along easily, but we crave and cry out for His goodness through comfort, guidance, wisdom, and peace as we're walking through valleys.

If you don't believe God is good, you'll never be able to walk in wild freedom, because you'll always be afraid of God. You won't have a holy fear (awe) of God's power and goodness, but you'll just be plain afraid that He's a capricious bully who is out to teach you a lesson.

Look at your life and see if you can look at the days to come and laugh. Do you believe that God wants good for you? Do you believe He *is* good? If there isn't fruit of that belief in your life, it's time to root out the poison that keeps you from experiencing life to the full. Ask God to show you His goodness. Take a careful look at Scripture to see how He points you to it. And then *expect* it.

My favorite way to learn to laugh at the days to come is to read biographies about and essays from women who lived in a time when life wasn't so comfortable. Women from past centuries encountered sickness and death regularly, but they still believed God was good and wanted good for them. In fact, they often leaned on Him with an intimate acquaintance. This is a huge faith-building exercise for me, and I return to it every time I start to wonder how much I can really trust God.

She overcomes through God's power.

The sting of death is sin, and the strength of sin is the law. But thanks be to God, who gives us the victory through our Lord Jesus Christ. Therefore, my beloved brethren, be stead-fast, immovable, always abounding in the work of the Lord, knowing that your labor is not in vain in the Lord.

1 Corinthians 15:56–58 NKJV

God is always moving in our lives. He promises to sanctify us; He's not just leaving us to labor to no avail. He gives us the Holy Spirit to spur us on and change us. We are no longer slaves to sin; we are set free in Christ.

Freedom feels uncomfortable sometimes, because the rules are stripped away. We have to rely on relationship over a set list of manufactured to-dos. That can be incredibly alarming because we have no way of measuring our goodness anymore. However, God says that Christ's goodness is our goodness. It is not our goodness that has any worth. In fact, it is only Christ's goodness and strength that have any power in our lives.

However, we get to join in the work of God and His saints. He invites us to play a part in making disciples in the whole world, in bringing heaven down to earth, and in bringing justice and mercy to pass. He will give us a supernatural ability to do these things in His timing and in His power. We don't have to strive. It is not a have-to but a get-to. Our identity and position are secure and hidden in Him, but our joy can be in joining Him in His work in the world. He will mold us and change us as we take steps of freedom. He will help us up when we topple over, off balance. He will give us strength when we're weary, and He will be our friend when we are lonely. His goodness is our goodness.

It's time to live bravely. It's time to believe that God isn't finished changing you. You don't have to be ashamed of where you are, because He's working in your heart and shifting the way you see things. He is mighty in you, and you are hidden in Him.

She is free from disappointment.

I press on toward the goal to win the prize for which God has called me heavenward in Christ Jesus.

Philippians 3:14

We know that not everything goes our way. If you've had a sibling or spent any time in school or failed to get a promotion, you know this is true. There is no way to tend to day-to-day life and not be tinged by the way the world falls short of our expectations. That's the thing. The whole world is broken, but God is making it new.

He won't let the world flounder forever in its sin.

He is making all things new, and He has already given us His Son and His Spirit, who are the solution to our inborn sin and the balm for our souls. We already have the prize, so we can be freed from the disappointments that come from dwelling in this crumbling, beautiful place.

We have to walk in the understanding that the world is broken and will disappoint us. People are hurting and will let us down and bang us up. But Jesus has already come and overcome and sent His Holy Spirit to comfort us in our suffering. He is already here with us, and He is perfect. He is the prize.

We don't have to live in the sting of the world's shortfalls, because we have the prize of Jesus Christ dwelling with us here, even amid the hurt and disappointment. You can love with abandon because your hope isn't in being loved back. You can hope in really big ways because God is a really big God. If He has already done the hard work of creating the world and reconciling us to Himself, do you trust that He is working still today?

She is content and rejects comparison, knowing she's free to walk as God has made her.

The fear of the LORD leads to life;
then one rests content, untouched by trouble.

Proverbs 19:23

The young lions suffer want and hunger;
but those who seek the LORD lack no good thing.

Psalm 34:10 ESV

The boundary lines have fallen for me in pleasant places;
surely I have a delightful inheritance.

Psalm 16:6

There are two cycles I've witnessed in my years of friendship with women. When we live by grace, we are grateful and gracious with others. When we're tempted to live by the law, we measure ourselves against others' value. When we are constantly measuring ourselves, we can't help but measure and critique others as well.

This is a graceless way of living and causes our spirit to be uncharitable toward others.

My friend Rose is the kind of girl most girls want to be. She's gregarious, gorgeous, smart, successful—and she's her own worst critic. I've known her since college, when she was a beautiful, high-achieving freshman. She was taking the campus by storm, and every guy wanted to know her.

But deep inside, she lived a small life chained by comparison. She was wound tight and deeply wanted control. That control ended up being over her body, and she wrestled her weight into submission. On the outside, she was all achievement and accolades. But on the inside, she was hurting deeply due to an eating disorder.

But in the ten years since college, I've gotten to watch Rose really open up and move past the small and scared life of her past. She's still the same gregarious and charming Rose, but she isn't wrestling with the beast of measuring up anymore. She believes the Lord made her good, on purpose, and for His glory. She believes in His goodness and His plan for her life.

This is what Rose told me when she described a free woman: "She knows herself and exudes confidence. She loves the person God created her to be. A free woman does not feel the need or desire to judge other women, and she doesn't feel so insecure that others are judging her. She *rests*, breathes, lives, and loves in His promises and truth."

She is not paralyzed by decisions, because she's indwelled with the Spirit of peace.

May the God of hope fill you with all joy and peace as you trust in him, so that you may overflow with hope by the power of the Holy Spirit.

Romans 15:13

My grandpa is a good man who taught me how to make decisions I can live with. He has always told me, "You make the best decision you can with what you know at the time, and then you move forward knowing you did what you could." This has saved me from years of second-guessing and allows me to make quick decisions I can live with. The beautiful thing is that for believers, this earthly wisdom is also coupled with the Holy Spirit of peace, who allows us to connect with the heart of God.

When we know Him, we're anchored to him. We can't swing too far off, because He'll bring us back to Himself.

Imagine this: You're in a giant room with a huge pendulum. The wire is attached securely at the ceiling, but the pendulum is free to swing as it pleases. Here's the truth: If something is attached at a point above it, it can only swing so far before it comes back to rest plumb with its support. I rest in this beautiful truth when I fear I'm going off script with the Lord. I know He's going to pursue me and that the Holy Spirit will guide and convict me.

We have free will, but we are also His. We are tethered to Him, and if we'll allow it, we'll always come back to His center.

She is not frantic, because God has numbered her days and guided her footsteps.

> In their hearts humans plan their course,
>> but the LORD establishes their steps.
>>>> *Proverbs 16:9*

> Your eyes saw my unformed body;
>> all the days ordained for me were written in your book
>> before one of them came to be.
>>>> *Psalm 139:16*

We are God's handiwork, created in Christ Jesus to do good
works, which God prepared in advance for us to do.

Ephesians 2:10

God has made me with ambition. I grew up on the older end
of the spectrum of millennials and was told again and again that I
could accomplish great things. My father was a feminist of sorts,
and he always encouraged me to be daring. His guidance gave me
high hopes and the feeling that few doors were closed to me.

However, when I became a Christian, I perceived that ambition was frowned on. Regardless of the why, it felt like when I
accepted Christ, I also laid down the part of my personality that
longed to achieve. This didn't stop my striving heart, though; I
simply funneled my ambition into "holier pursuits" such as serving
and mothering.

As the firstborn of high-achieving parents, I was gifted with a
nonstop motor and a desire to please at birth. I felt like if I wasn't
moving, work wasn't getting done. In my early adulthood, this
swung from a healthy work ethic to an anxious frenzy. I truly
believed I was responsible for keeping the world spinning.

But that was never God's intention for me or for you. He is
the Lord. He sits on the throne. He is actually the one who set
the world in motion, and He doesn't need our help to keep it on
its axis.

Ephesians 2:10 lets us in on a little secret: God has already
prepared your good works ahead of time, before you were born.
You must just walk forward in them, hand in hand with Him. He
is a good father and best friend. He is a trusted counselor who will
guide your steps.

*She is filled with the Holy Spirit, so she's able to love as He loves,
without restraint.*

The fruit of the Spirit is love, joy, peace, forbearance, kindness, goodness, faithfulness, gentleness and self-control. Against such things there is no law.

Galatians 5:22–23

No man knows how bad he is till he has tried very hard to be good.

C. S. Lewis, Mere Christianity

Here's the deal: There is a word I have come to adore in the English language. I've been enamored by the idea and sound of *charity* for years—the virtue that allows us to think well of people. *Charity* means "kindness, goodwill, and consideration in judging others." It's imperative that we learn to think well of others. Sure, they're sinful, but they're made in the image of your God.

We shouldn't walk around believing that others are out to get us or hurt us. To believe that is to believe a lie from the enemy, hoping you'll distance yourself from other people. Because God loves us, we're able to love without restraint. As believers, we have been forgiven so much that to withhold charity from someone feels so graceless and cold. We can do better than that. We can preemptively love people with the warmth and care with which our heavenly Father preemptively loved us. We can live winsomely, because people who are truly charitable in spirit are magnetic.

When we interpret each other through the lens of generosity, graciousness, and kindness, we are trusting that the Holy Spirit is at work and that Christ has already overcome.

She is steadfast in her call, knowing her great weakness, tied only to God.

Now he has reconciled you by Christ's physical body through death to present you holy in his sight, without blemish and free from accusation—if you continue in your faith, established and firm, and do not move from the hope held out in the gospel.

Colossians 1:22–23

Grace is countercultural and strips us of our worldly rules and goalposts, so we are pushed to be nearer to the Lord moment by moment. This is deeply unsettling in a world that loves to measure. Businesspeople often pass around the quote, "You cannot manage what you cannot measure." This is modern-day gospel for the do-it-all, obsessed culture we live in.

It may be true for organizations and businesses, but it is not true for the Christian life, and you will kill yourself (or others) with condemnation if you try. If you begin to measure the health of your spiritual life by a set of external indicators, you're destined for disappointment or exhaustion. Only our relationship with the Lord and knowing His love for us and His good news will compel us to good works and steadfast heart change.

We can stay in the hope of the gospel when we stay near to the Lord. This works itself out in different ways for different people in different seasons, but it can't be boiled down to a simple checklist.

She is unbound from final fear.

"This sickness will not end in death."

John 11:4

For the longest time, even after becoming a believer, I struggled with the idea of death. I feared heaven, and an eternity sounded like an awfully long time. A large part of my struggle was the belief that nothing could be better than the life I was living now.

To be honest, I have seen people deal with the idea of eternity differently. My six-year-old, Cooper, often asks me to climb into the top bunk at night. He wants me to talk to him about dying and heaven. I get the sense that he wants me to persuade him of the goodness to come. He wants to know what it will be like. Will he get to be with us? Will he still be himself? I can feel the fear drain from him as his eyes grow heavy, but this only comes after lots of words about the goodness of God and how in heaven we'll be free from fear and pain.

On the flip side, my husband's grandparents have been faithful servants for decades. They love the Lord and have followed Him for as long as they remember. As their bodies age and their friends die, and as they sense more brokenness in the world, their hope is in death, as it was for the apostle Paul, who wrote, "To me, to live is Christ and to die is gain" (Philippians 1:21)—because of Christ. Paul was really speaking in paradox, because he was saying if he stays alive here on earth, great! He'll still get to be in service of the Lord. However, if he dies on earth, he'll be raised in eternity and will be in intimate communion with the Lord.

This disease of sin and brokenness that started at the first bite of off-limits fruit from the tree of the knowledge of good and evil is not terminal. This disease will not end in death, but you'll be raised with all the saints. That feels like such a great comfort, a balm when you're afraid. This disease that we inherited is not the end of us. It will not take us down; it will not bury us. We'll be raised with Christ.

This kind of freedom allows you to step out of defensive living. You can cheer wildly as you're unchained from the fear, sin, and shame that have hindered you. As you walk more and more freely, you're less tethered to earthly things. You're able to love better, live more engaged, and run more closely with the Lord. This is all wildly good news.

PRAYER

Father, help us live like women who are unchained and unafraid. We don't have to live as though Jesus never died and rose again. He not only died, but He broke the chains of death, forever ending its power. Lord, be with us as we learn to walk in the freedom that's already ours. Help us to learn Your goodness, and help us to live fearlessly. Help us to believe that You're daily changing us to be more like Your Son. Help us to not live afraid that we're going to go off course, because we know we're tethered to You, Lord—and only You.

JESS'S RESPONSE

Watching Hayley these past few years has been such a beautiful catalyst for me to pursue freedom in my own life, to ask the Lord to show me the places that are very much locked up and in bondage.

The biggest thing I've found is that as I'm walking out the liberty that was won for me on the cross, action is almost always required. Indecision is never free. Freedom from body insecurity for me means exercising often, not believing the lie, "There's no point. Just stay home!" Freedom from striving often means diving into rest in a truly active way—hiding my phone, canceling plans, and saying no. Freedom from comparison takes action—praying for the women I compare myself to, lifting them up and encouraging them when I can, and verbally thanking God for the pleasant lines He's drawn for me.

The Danger of Staying Tame

One night, Hayley and I were out with friends enjoying dinner, answering questions about our upcoming book, when a friend's husband made a little joke about something silly I'd said. "Oh, so you're obviously the wild one," he said, laughing from across the table. I can't for the life of me remember what I'd said that seemed a little pushy or punchy, but I can remember that was the exact moment I started feeling insecure about how people would interpret *wild*. Up until that moment, in the early stages of talking to people about our book idea, the phrase "wild and free" felt very sacred. Hayley and I would trade it back and forth in text messages or when praying for one another. It was a confession of knowing that God wanted more and a prayer for immeasurably more than we could ask or imagine. I'd spoken to my husband, and he'd nodded without reservation. I'd told the idea to my mom, who didn't bat an eyelash—but she did tear up as she resonated with the idea. No one and nothing had caused me to feel insecure about the word *wild* until that night.

And you know? I totally get it. I mentioned in chapter 1 that I'd like to redeem the word *wild*, and I stand by that. Our culture has diluted it, and now it muddily seems sinful, wicked, selfish, and reckless. The kind of wild the world sees is *not* our wild. Our wild doesn't mean driving with no regard for the rules of the road. It doesn't mean TV shows that exploit college girls who are looking for love and acceptance. It doesn't mean subverting the system, living on the far edge of legal boundaries, or paving your own way while thumbing your nose at The Man.

When we look at the word in the context of creation—more specifically, in the context of creatures and their Creator—the vision for what is truly wild takes on a new light. It's beautiful and freeing, and it is much more about relationship than it is about rebellion. A wild woman is unhindered by cultural norms, "fitting in," or what's taking place around her. She is in her most natural state. She isn't wild because she is tough or pushy or has an ultra-strong will. She is wild because she is inextricably rooted in the strongest One. She is wild in *His* strength, not her own.

So I propose we redeem the word and make peace with it all at once. If you've felt like too much and that *wild* has been placed on you like a scarlet letter, let's take it gently to Jesus and ask Him to speak identity over us. Let's not allow memories or descriptions from others to be our identity makers. If you've felt like surely you're not enough and that you'd never in a million years live up to the description of *wild*, let's remember that you already are wild. You were made wild in your creation and restored in salvation; it's nothing you have to put on or muster up.

Yes, our culture will likely keep their working definition of what they see as "wild." I think our best option for coping with this misunderstanding is to smile over the table when we're mis-understood. We can pour grace on the world that wants to twist the words God has created to identify us. We know it's not really about us, so we'll redeem *wild* by keeping our eyes on Jesus as we live out what we've been called to as best we can—allowing *wild* to look holy and full of life as we move forward. We'll change the perception by living wild in the power of the Holy Spirit, forgiven by the work of Jesus when He died on the cross for our sins, under the watchful and loving approval of our Father God.

Our culture says loudly and clearly that there are two ways to win affection: First, *fit in*. Go the same way everyone else is going; take the next practical step; look like the other moms do; don't skip a year between high school and college; use the same diaper brands your friends do; feel free to have burdens as long as they don't ruffle too many feathers; know when to be quiet. There is even pressure to interpret Scripture and respond to the Lord in the exact same way as those around us. Second, *stand out*. Don't just accept the status quo; don't believe everything you're told—find out for yourself; break the mold; be special, unique, and brave; fight for your rights; set your own course; do what your heart tells you to do; question everything; do what's right for you.

And what is the call of the woman set wild and free in God? Her eyes are on Jesus. He determines her path, and she trusts Him. She isn't concerned with fitting in *or* standing out, since her identity is in step with her Father. She knows better than to expect to be tidy and put together, since that is not her aim—but she also doesn't feel an ounce of pressure to be set apart from the crowd. She would point any attention offered to her Father, anyhow. Her hands are open. Her rights are relinquished. She holds the staff of the daughter of the Most High God and believes Isaiah 54:17, which tells her that no weapon forged against her will prevail, and Romans 8:37, which tells her that she is more than a conqueror through Christ.

The world can get hung up on the word *wild* and what it means to them—and anytime they want, the world can throw a big side eye at the woman set wild and free in God. She doesn't live for them; she sees only her Father.

The Tension of Tolerance

One of my mom's side ministries used to be sharing the gospel with nail salon workers. I remember the times I'd accompany her to get a fill-in or an occasional pedicure. I could absolutely count on her witnessing and sharing Jesus with the person doing her nails. They were totally captive, superclose in proximity—so why not just go in and offer them some hope, right? I've taken after my mom in many beautiful ways, and I do really like to get my nails done, but I'm bummed to say I haven't taken up her mantle of nail salon ministry.

I excuse myself by pointing to my intense introversion and the fact that I'm a pastor's wife who just needs an afternoon off every once in a while. I've yet to use my headphones when I get my nails done, but I've been close. I go in, keep to myself, read a few magazines, get a fresh coat of black, and get out.

This weekend, however, I got called up to the front lines. I was just there, minding my business, zoning out as I watched this sweet gal layer on my beloved dark polish, when she just asked me out of the blue, "Do you believe in God?" What a ginormous and beautiful question. I said, "Yes, I do believe in God"—and specifically that I believe in having a relationship with Jesus. She began to share her thoughts about what she believes and what she's heard, and I'm so bummed to tell you that a lot of it was man-made junk. It was a mix of independent character building with a few dashes of reincarnation. It sounded so hard, like so much burden and personal responsibility, and it made me exhausted and scared on her behalf all at once.

As I responded to her thoughts, she said something so striking. "It doesn't seem to make you mad that I don't believe what you believe." Make me mad? Huh? I told her gently that it didn't make me mad in the slightest. It burdened me for her and made me sad for the heavy load she seemed to be carrying. Her beliefs, however broken, don't infringe on me or hurt me, and I certainly don't think I'm any better than she is, based on my own merits, because it is God who poured some lavish grace on me and let me distinguish light from dark when I was fifteen. I left broken for her, praying for her—and later that night, I spent time with my kids praying for her.

But she touched on an issue for our generation and our current culture of Christianity. We have massively mixed up what it means to be tolerant and what it means to be tame. We struggle with knowing how to effectively tolerate other viewpoints and simultaneously love people well. How do we accept their beliefs and practices, even when they go so firmly against what we see as right and true in God's Word? How and when do we draw a line in the sand and say, "No—no, we can't let this go down"? The tension has created quite the chasm, and you may know firmly which side you're on, or you may be like me—hovering with a foot on each side, fairly certain you're about to be split into two.

It seems that one side of Christian culture says we cannot or should not tolerate the community around us walking in a way that feels contrary to our convictions. It's terrifying to see our world going to hell in a handbasket, and it seems the only way to fight is to separate and hide, judge and draw lines. That side believes we should love the world, but we should love them toward believing what we believe and living how we live, because that is God's best for all of us. I resonate with this side sometimes. I genuinely do. I read truth in God's Word and I believe it; I live it out and don't feel conflicted or boxed in by God—I feel set free by His commandments. I feel safe in His statutes. But I know that until most people experience the liberty of the Holy Spirit grabbing their heart and making it new, "living for God" doesn't feel like freedom.

The other side of Christian culture is tired of hurting the rest of the world and wounding them with our judgment. They're tired of making those who aren't walking with Christ feel "less than" or unseen. They want to hear individual stories and experiences rather than make blanket assumptions about what is right for everyone based on what they read in the Bible. And yet, the lines get a little more muddied every day as culture progresses and we get further from the time when God's Word was written. Sometimes it's hard to see what marks this camp as being compelled and controlled by the love of God. I resonate with these guys too. I don't want to tell my friend I met at yoga that I think she is going to hell because of what she believes, and I don't want to tell my barista that he needs to change everything about his life before he's *really* welcome at my church, when I know God created him as good—with a plan for his life.

But where does tolerance point us? Does tolerance mean we let others live as they want, let the world progress as it is, hide away, shout at them that they're wrong, and hope that somehow that changes things? Does tolerance have wide-open arms that indicate it's totally OK to believe what you believe? Would loving tolerance allow the rest of the world to live as it wishes in order to keep the peace, even if we know it might not be abundant life for them?

The beautiful—and surprising—answer is that tolerance isn't a man-made concept, it's a God-breathed one. We can look to His Word for answers rather than battling it out ourselves. First, let's look at how the world defines tolerance.

The Random House Dictionary defines tolerance as "a fair, objective, and permissive attitude toward those whose opinions, practices, race, religion, nationality, etc., differ from one's own: freedom from bigotry." It also defines it as "interest in and concern for ideas, opinions, practices, etc., foreign to one's own." But by far, my favorite definition is this: "the act or capacity of enduring." When we put these together, I feel like the scales begin to fall off my eyes and I can breathe a little more easily.

Tolerance is seeing people fairly, objectively, permissively.

Taking interest in and showing concern for what they believe, even when their beliefs are different from my beliefs? Yes. I can do that. And even more so—the idea that tolerating is the capacity to endure. I know I can do that because it's exactly how I see my Jesus live and love in the Bible. I see a lot of Him calling people to life and truth. I see a lot of Him asking them to repent and give up their brokenness. But I also see days, weeks, and years of Him walking with sinners—with men and women whose practices and opinions were so majorly off. I see Him caring, expressing concern, and, mostly, I see Him enduring. Loving. All the way to the cross.

Tolerance is no longer a scary word to me, no longer a chasm of misunderstanding that I'm worried I will fall into. I remember that 2 Timothy 4:2 says to preach the word, but to do it with complete patience. Ephesians 4:2 reminds me that my call is to walk in humility and gentleness, with patience, bearing with people in love. Romans 2:4 asks, "Do you show contempt for the riches of his kindness, forbearance and patience, not realizing that God's kindness is intended to lead you to repentance?" I'm compelled by that question to remember how great God's tolerance and patience are with *me* and how He equips me to keep sharing them with others. I can picture Jesus' face in John 8 when he told any onlooker who was sinless to throw the first stone, and I can see the intensity in Paul's eyes when he reminds his people in Romans 16 to be careful of those who teach untruths that cause division.

There is tension in tolerance, but the amazing news is that our Father thrives in human tension. That is where He does His most unexpected work. He brings lightness to heavy burdens, and the Holy Spirit brings wisdom whenever we ask for it. At the foot of the cross, we are wild and free women. We can hold love and truth equally in our hands. We can be passionate and tolerant; we can be truth tellers while being loving and patient like Jesus is. We can walk with Jesus and watch how He loves.

Being Tame Is Dangerous

There is so much opportunity for us once we view tolerance from Jesus' perspective, but there is also challenge when we consider the idea of being tame from a kingdom viewpoint. In chapter 1, I shared about seeing the documentary on the wild horses of Corolla. Since I'm only a few hours' drive from them, I naturally became fascinated with the phenomenon and began doing research on how and where to see them. The most interesting thing I found was the restrictions on what you're allowed to do and not do in relation to the horses. Since I've never really encountered any truly wild animals larger than the weird possum that hangs around my house at night, I didn't realize just how steadfast the community around the horses must be to keep them truly wild.

While the surrounding communities offer tours to see the horses and are proud of the value they bring, stringent laws are in place to protect them. It is illegal to feed them in any way. This statute isn't in place for the safety of the humans as much as for the horses. In my research, I read that even one tamed horse—even one animal that becomes slightly dependent on humans for food in any way—can endanger the rest of the species. If even one of the herd begins acting in a way that is no longer wild, the rest will follow suit, and the entire wild species will become extinct.

When humans come and go, build buildings, and create a culture around them, the horses are unaffected. You can pay to go on a tour and stay at a reasonable distance, and they will go about their business. The horses are tolerant to these changes around them. They are able to endure the changes as they come. But they are not tamed. No matter what shifts around them, they stay true to their identity of wild freedom.

I fear that we as women have spent so much energy sifting out what it looks like to be tolerant that we have forgotten the incredibly real threat of becoming tame ourselves. We have forgotten who is the source of our life, our hope, our encouragement. We have taken the bait and the idols the world offers us, because they're easy and pleasing and then we don't have to wait on our Abba provider.

When culture tells us we must look a certain way, we obey. If it tells us it's "normal" and "responsible" to have a savings fund and 401(k), we respond. When we're confronted with the typical outline of how the rest of the world believes our lives should go, we see no reason to be the odd girl out. If everyone else has a two-car garage, why wouldn't we? If the world says we need a certain phone to stay in sync, then by all means, get it. When confronted with the changing civilization around us, I'm sad to say I don't see many Christian women, myself included, fighting the status quo. Rather, I see myself and women like me responding. We may not always meet the expectations of those around us, but we certainly try. At the least, we feel the pressure to do so, even when we stand strong and refuse to give in to some things.

Throughout the writing of *Wild and Free*, Hayley and I have taken to social media to hear from real women about how they interact with some of these ideas. Mostly we want to hear what wild and free looks like to them so we're not sharing only our perspective. In the writing of this chapter, I asked a different and more personal question on Facebook—I asked if any women would be willing to share a story of living tame. Here's what I heard:

"There was a time in my life a few years ago when I lived completely turned inward, folded into fear. What began as mundane, daily worries escalated to a full-blown panic so intense that I avoided leaving my house or going out at night. I knew in my head the truth about God and who He was inside me, but freedom—living wildly in my identity as a beloved daughter of God—seemed more like a far-off destination. Because I didn't know the freedom Christ had *already* died for, I couldn't share it with others. I lived tame, fruitless, choked by worry. My actions reflected what my mind thought about: *Protect yourself—God isn't for you.*"

"Three summers ago, I met a great guy. We dated, and it was lovely. And I quickly paid attention to his dreams and calling. And I was ready to make them mine. I was ready to stop having my own dreams, to rest comfortably in his instead of my own."

"A major time I lived what I consider to be tame was when I found myself so deeply entrenched in the church culture/bubble that I realized I had never spoken to my actual neighbors. I also didn't have any friends I didn't go to church with! I was so afraid of having my shaky faith questioned that I just played it safe. Definitely tame, for sure! Thankfully that is in the past, and the Lord has grown my confidence in Him, and I have lovely friends and neighbors very far out of my church bubble to have fun with!"

If the definition of tolerance was a little freeing and life-giving, the definition of tame was, for me, gripping and convicting. *The Random House Dictionary* defines the word *tame* in a number of ways, including "changed from the wild . . . state; lacking in excitement; dull; insipid; spiritless; not to be taken very seriously; without real power or importance; brought into service, rendered useful and manageable; under control."

I confess, even as I write this chapter, I feel separated from the wild state that I am calling other women to. I know in my head that I am wild, and I know in my heart that I am free—but my flesh so often just wants to fit in. And how many times have

I bemoaned the lack of excitement in my life, only because I'm choosing not to walk in the joy of the season God has called me to? Because I am looking longingly at those around me, wishing I could be just a little more like them or have the adventure their lives seem to have? *O Father, forgive me for often living a Spiritless life by listening more to my own voice than that of the Holy Ghost Helper You sent to be my guide. Forgive me for doing things in my own strength and my own power rather than letting myself be weak so that You can be strong in me.*

I don't even need to worry about the other people who don't take me seriously, because so often I don't take myself seriously. I'm more likely to wake up and see my faults and needs than to wake up and remind myself that I'm a part of a holy nation, a member of a royal priesthood (1 Peter 2:9), called to share about the marvelous light that changed my life. Maybe I shrug when people ask me what my spiritual gifts are rather than glorifying God by owning the mission He's given me and the tools He's equipped me with to get me where He wants me to go.

And sadly, I know what it means to be brought into service and live under the control of someone other than my King and Father. I've frequently walked away from the beautiful and freeing relationship with God to tether myself to addictions, idols, and even my own afflictions. I've been owned by my injuries and ailments, I've been owned by my relationships, and I've been rendered useful and manageable for the prince of this world, the enemy of my soul.

But today, for me and for you, I say, "No more."

Today I remember and remind you that Jesus died so we might not be tame any longer. We are still the wild women He created, and He has never stopped longing to give us all we need. He has never stopped *being* all we need. He comes in and makes our days and lives mean something. He brings all the joy and excitement—more than we could ask or imagine. Our Father has taken us seriously, so much so that He sent His most loved Son to the cross to die on our behalf. And moreover, I declare and celebrate that we are no longer slaves to sin; we are wild and free daughters of God.

Protect the Herd

Can you see how the timidity of just one woman might endanger the generations? One woman stops believing that God will provide all her needs, that God Himself is enough for her needs, and thus all the women struggle with the same belief. When one woman decides that some parts of the abundant life God has promised must not be for her—she can so easily speak that into the women around her. When she doubts her worth in Him, her calling in Him, her redemption in Him—those kinds of timid thoughts can seep into the cracks of community, maiming the ministry He has for those women on a whole.

You know how women hit that year in their lives when their metabolism miraculously slows down? I say miraculously, not because it's good, but because it seems almost otherworldly. One day you're a young little thing who can eat her weight in pizza and work out for funsies, and the next day you can't look at a carrot stick without having to run a mile to work it off. I hit that time kind of early, around my freshman year of college. I'd always had a basic insecurity about my body, and I'd always known I was a bit heavier than all my friends, but that was pretty much it.

And then that awful metabolism death happened. Suddenly my slightly overweight self was very literally obese. I was shocked at the number on the scale when I finally weighed myself, and I was ashamed, frustrated, angry, and instantly insecure. After a while, I turned to health and fitness for help, but first I took all my intense pain and let it metastasize into pride and judgment on others. That's normal, right?

When confronted with my unhealthy life and patterns, instead of working on my health, I set my sights on covering up my unhealthy body and became freakishly passionate about modesty. If you don't know how to fix the problem, just cover it up, right?

Even though I lived in the middle of South Carolina, where it's basically 100 degrees on pleasant days, I refused to wear shorts or short sleeves. I told people it was because God was correcting me and teaching me about modesty and really honoring my body, but secretly, I was living completely in bondage to body insecurity.

I shudder to think about how many women I preached my extreme modesty propaganda to. I was a high school youth leader at the time, so you can imagine I was just a bundle of joy for those young girls to deal with. The point is this: My timidity was absolutely used as a tool of the enemy against the freedom of other women.

You've probably seen some version of this before, on some scale, in your past and maybe even now in your present. One woman decides her beauty isn't up to par and becomes obsessed with diet and exercise. A few other women get caught up into that process by association, and soon a whole community is waving the flag of health higher than they wave the flag of Jesus. Maybe one woman struggles with fear or anxiety over her safety, and it incites widespread concern about encountering strangers. A newcomer doesn't make her excited but makes her cautious, and over time, a whole group of women learns to distrust and shun visitors. One gal in a group of single girls gets obsessed with marriage and stops trusting God for the time when she'll meet her husband-to-be. Suddenly they all become insecure about not being married yet. Maybe just one or two women in a community forget that speaking life is the first language of their Father, and they start an avalanche of gossip flowing through the whole group. The point is, tame living spreads most often with one woman trading in her freedom and her identity at a time.

Unfortunately, I've been the leading lady in this sad scenario before. I've been the one inhibited by another woman's lack of freedom as well, but the times when I've been the frontrunner of captivity stick out more in my mind. Because of that, I thank God for His great grace that covers us and for His great grace that spurs us on to put a stop to this broken phenomenon. The beautiful difference between us and those wild horses is that when we act tame, we don't have to be removed, and the damage is never irreversible. We have our words; we have grace; and we have the power of the Holy Spirit to help us to begin again. We can apologize, correct our mistakes, ask for grace, and swim in the freedom that comes with God's mercy. Moreover, we don't have to live in fear of what our lack of freedom will cause in light of community when we live out our mission to spread the wild and free identity we've been given.

Sisters, we don't need to shrink back from loving those who are different from us. And we don't have to settle for a tame existence either. God's wild freedom compels as we seek to love others, and it unchains us as we live out His love for us.

PRAYER

Father, give us eyes to see the parts of our lives where we've bought lies about who we are and whose we are. Help us to see that the actual call of wild women has nothing to do with strong personalities and everything to do with a strong God. In Jesus' great name, we hold up our hands and confess we've confused what it means to be tolerant and what it means to be tame. We want to watch how Jesus loves and endures and to also hold fast to the identities You gave us and not submit to the yokes of slavery we've been freed from. Give us eyes to see and ears to hear and hearts ready to apologize, give grace, and walk in healing in Your name. Thank You for holding us and spurring us on for the sake of Your kingdom.

We love You.

Love, Your wild girls

HAYLEY'S RESPONSE

It's hard to know how to handle the things that oppose what God seems to be about in Scripture but absolutely love the child we *know* He loves from reading Scripture. We hear the word *tolerance* all the time these days, and it seems that Christians are the number-one offenders in the lack-of-tolerance department. I think Jess is right—we've been sold a false bill of goods about what tolerance really means.

The church has not always done a great job of informing this discussion either. But let's be long-suffering women. Let's be the kind of women who believe no one is too unreachable for God. Let's trust the Father has room to work and also has a little mystery left up His sleeve.

I pray we'll move collectively into a place where we believe this seventeenth-century motto: "In essentials unity, in nonessentials liberty, in all things charity."

When We Prefer Captivity

Even as I've learned to walk more wildly and freely, there are days when it all feels like a lot. There are days when I'd like to slink back to my old defensive living. I'd love to go on autopilot and let my innate tendencies take over again. Sometimes the old patterns feel comforting, even if they also feel rotten.

Fortunately, I'm not the only one struggling with the pull of living small and scared. Even such heroes of the faith as Moses felt this way:

> Then Moses turned to the LORD and said, "O LORD, why have you done evil to this people? Why did you ever send me? For since I came to Pharaoh to speak your name, he has done evil to this people, and you have not delivered your people at all."
>
> *Exodus 5:22–23 ESV*

Moses had a personal call and encounter with the Lord, but he questioned why God had him fighting for freedom. And how often do we do this? We know that God is a champion of freedom, but we question why He has us fighting for it. And it is simple: We fight for freedom because God wants us not to be indebted or indentured to anyone but Him.

The building of the song of freedom often feels like a burden. It feels like this hope of freedom is right in a really true way. It is good and right and real, deep down in your bones. Sometimes it feels like the only right thing you know.

But getting from where you are to the point of being free can feel impossible.

Why We Prefer Captivity

At times, we miss or prefer captivity. Sure, wild and free sounds great—but sometimes we're tempted to look back to the way life used to be. We moan about what we left behind, missing the trappings of how we used to live. We even begrudge the daily provision God gives us, like the Israelites who whined about the manna God rained down every day. I can just imagine them stomping their feet and remembering their slavery with a rosy filter of nostalgia: "Maybe things weren't so bad there after all. At least we were taken care of. We weren't stuck in the wilderness. We knew what to expect."

It's not surprising we would cling to what we know and see, that we would reject God's lavish, manna-like provision, that we would want to go it alone and march ourselves right back into the familiar bondage.

At this point, it's pretty clear that freedom is an important and worthy pursuit. Galatians 5:1 tells us it is *for* freedom that Christ set us free. However, there are times when we actually prefer captivity, much like our flesh prefers self and sin. We'd never want our friends or our daughters to live in bondage or captivity or anything other than the lush and wild freedom of God. Why is it, then, that we prefer the cage ourselves?

The boundaries are clear. We've been conditioned to desire boundaries since we were children. We were told to stand in lines to go to the bathroom at school. We held hands and looked both ways when crossing the street. We quickly learned to color within the lines and to not break crayons and to play nicely with others.

In school, we move into getting grades to measure our performance. In exercise, in work, and even in church, we are a culture obsessed with strategy and measurement.

We all learn to live by the rules of our captivity. Our habits are comforting, even if they keep us from God's best. We often self-soothe with the things that hold us in bondage. They are the things, habits, or people we go to instead of relying solely on the Lord.

Operating in freedom can feel chaotic. We are stripped of our measuring stick, our goalposts, and the world's promises. We are left simply with the knowledge that when we are in Christ, we are His and we are free. We are pushed to intimacy with the Spirit instead of a set of to-dos or measurements. We are left to do business with a God who is invisible but omnipresent.

When my son Cooper was learning how to ride a bike, he desperately wanted his training wheels. Even though he knew my husband had his hand on the seat the whole time, Cooper didn't *feel* safe. Cooper missed how the training wheels made him feel steady and secure, how they kept him level to the ground. But with Mike's hand on the back of the bike, Cooper was safer than he was with the training wheels. Cooper had his father's whole attention, guiding and steadying him as he worked the pedals and the handlebars.

It was a wobbly start, accompanied by tears and frustration. Even though Mike's hand was steadying the bike, because Mike was behind Cooper, Cooper often had a hard time believing he was there. It took a long time for Cooper to find his balance and to learn how to pedal while steering and balancing. It seemed like it took forever for him to realize that the more he relaxed, the easier it all really was. After every spill, I could see Cooper's eyes move to where the training wheels used to be. He longed mostly for the feeling of security—that he was safe, that things were predictable.

Learning how to ride a bike is unpredictable business. It's hard work to learn to trust physics (a force you experience but cannot see). It's hard work to learn to trust the way God has made your body, with the ability to do more than one thing at once. But once you learn how to ride that bike, you don't forget. And you gain incredible freedom.

Learning to love freedom is a lot like learning to ride a bike. It feels awkward and wobbly at first. If you're a perfectionist, it can be tempting to quit and to screw those training wheels right back on. It takes a lot of failing, a lot of skinning your knees and returning to the Lord for healing. But when you finally find the rhythm and balance of freedom, when you can have faith in the ways of God and the way He has made you, you can go so much further and see so many beautiful things.

Cooper loves to ride his bike now. He bops off the bus two steps at a time and begs to hop on his bike to cruise to the cul-de-sac down from our house. He's found his footing, and as his mother, I'm so blessed to watch and behold. What felt like forever to Cooper really only took a week or so. And now he has a lifetime of freedom ahead of him.

We know that God is wild, but He is thoroughly careful. Because He is all-knowing, He cannot be careless. Even when we feel unsure in our freedom, longing instead to cling to false fences and rules, He is still God. He hasn't changed, even if things feel chaotic to us. He will bring chaos into order.

It's easier to stay. After a while, captivity doesn't even feel so much like bondage, but more like an altered way of living. We get used to our confines and learn to live within the bounds. We can begin to be grateful for the safety of the walls we've found ourselves in, even if safety is just an illusion.

Stockholm syndrome, or capture bonding, is a strange psychological occurrence in which hostages express empathy and have positive feelings toward their captors, sometimes to the point of defending them. We can act this way about our captivity. Paul unpacks our tendency to put up with abuse in his letter to the Corinthian church: "*You put up with it* when someone enslaves you, takes everything you have, takes advantage of you, takes control of everything, and slaps you in the face" (2 Corinthians 11:20 NLT, emphasis mine).

But it's just another way of coping, of living defensively, to stay where you are clearly in bondage. Obviously, most of us do not endure being physically captured, but we're captured by our own proclivities all the time. We identify with our sin patterns and our unhealthy relationships to the point of having positive feelings toward them sometimes.

It may be tempting to believe that your desire for control is really just *being responsible*. Or maybe your shame feels so familiar you'd feel naked without it. Maybe you think your consuming fear will keep you safe. Whatever it is, staying wrapped up in your flesh will never allow you to be free.

But a lot of times it's easier to stay than to leave captivity. It is the path of least resistance. It takes calculated energy and heart focus to throw off the things that have been weighing you down.

We want to do it ourselves. I am the biggest do-it-yourselfer. The problem is, when you do it yourself and in your own power, you will only get what you can do. Ever. That is not the way of God. He wants to free us from what my author friend Emily Freeman calls the "try-hard life."

As creative entrepreneurs, my husband and I do not have the same stable and steady income situation we had when he worked a cushy corporate job. We have to depend daily on God's provision. When you have a steady paycheck coming from a big corporation, you can trick yourself into thinking you don't have to rely on God, but that's just your perception, a lie you're telling yourself, not reality. Now, in our life of self-employment, we very much have to quarterly, monthly, weekly, and daily depend on God's provision for our family.

There are days when our checking account dwindles and my husband expresses concern. Because we have the flexibility to pivot and change direction, I'll pull myself up by my good old Midwestern bootstraps and declare to Mike a new way I've thought of to make money. I'm an idea person—this is *always* my default. I want to do it myself, to produce, to go it alone. I don't want to have to depend in a submissive way on God to provide; I want to be assertive almost to the point of aggression.

It feels comforting to be in control, even when we have a sense that the control we're experiencing wouldn't hold up well if challenged. It's not always bad to make something happen, but if God is not the wind in those sails, if He isn't breathing life there, it will only lead to exhaustion and frustration. You will feel more battered and chained to your anxiety and despair than ever before.

It's easier to play the victim. Sometimes it feels comforting to be labeled as something. We readily accept labels for ourselves, just like we accept rules, regulations, measuring sticks, and to-dos. They give us a framework to tell how good or bad we're doing. If we remain victims of our circumstances, we can begin to both relish and resent our circumstances. We can believe the lie that we are our label.

Songwriter Lauren Daigle writes about this in "Come Alive (Dry Bones)":

> *Through the eyes of men it seems*
> *There's so much we have lost*
> *As we look down the road*
> *Where all the prodigals have walked*

And one by one
The enemy has whispered lies
And led them off as slaves
But we know that you are God
Yours is the victory
We know there is more to come
That we may not yet see
So with the faith you've given us
We'll step into the valley unafraid, yeah.[9]

This is the melody of leaving behind the lie of your label. You are not a screwup, but saved. You are not your disease, but a cared-for daughter. You are not the sum of the wounds you've been dealt, but a woman who is ripe for healing.

There is no reason to bear up under the burden of a label. You are victorious in Christ, and He has claimed that for you.

Why Freedom Is Better

Anything kept in captivity can only grow as much as its cage will allow. If we aren't walking out of our bondage, we're missing out on the fullness and on the abundant life of Christ.

Freedom is a gift from God, dependent on Christ. As we saw earlier, it is for freedom itself that God set us free. In Paul's letter to the Galatian church, he writes about how important maintaining freedom is, because he has seen how easily people walk right back into the yoke of bondage.

A group of people called Judaizers were preaching a message that sounded similar to the one Jesus had preached, but their message was fraught with extra requirements. They believed that to really accept Christ as the Messiah, a Gentile would first have to convert to Judaism. Paul fervently opposed this because it wasn't the gospel that Jesus preached.

Paul warned in Galatians 5:1–5 that the Judaizers would try to put a burden back on believers, a burden Christ Himself didn't require. These Judaizers were pharisaical and believed that Christians still had to follow old covenant law. There were a lot of "earning salvation" attitudes going on. This freaked Paul out because he saw how clearly God-prompted his own conversion was. John Piper said this about that kind of Judaizer thinking:

> [The gratitude ethic] tends to think of God's work for us as only in the past. It says, God *has* done so much for me, now I will do for Him. But this overlooks the fact that God's work for us is past, present, and future, *and* it is not only work *for* us but *in* us. The gratitude ethic tends to forget that apart from Christ's present indwelling power we can do nothing valuable (John 15:5). The gratitude ethic forgets that any patience, kindness, goodness, worship, etc., which we may offer to God is the fruit of *his* Spirit (Galatians 5:22; Philippians 3:3). It is God *now* working in us that which is pleasing in his sight (Hebrews 13:21). Therefore, even our gifts *to* God are gifts *from* God.[10]

Our freedom was bought on the cross, but that freedom is something we have to stand in daily. We can be tempted to believe we live as earners instead of daughters of the Lord. Galatians 5:4 (ESV) reads, "You are severed from Christ, you who would be justified by the law; you have fallen away from grace." We cannot try to be justified by the law, because we will fail and be found lacking; we can only trust in the grace and freedom of Christ.

God is our only hiding place, and He is sufficient. You don't have to find a box to hide in, because you are already hidden in the fullness of God. Colossians 3:3 states that once you accepted the Lord, "you died, and your life is now hidden with Christ in God." That is *really, really* good news. We don't have to hide; we don't have to surround ourselves with trappings; and we don't have to worry about being found out.

Corrie ten Boom was a gray-haired septuagenarian when someone first took interest in publishing an account of her wild life. She had helped hundreds of Jews find safe hiding places during the Holocaust because of her unending belief that God is good, loves us, and desires our freedom. She found the oppression of the Nazis abhorrent, even though as a Christian she was not being directly targeted. She looked evil in the eye and decided to take a stand against it.

The protection we thought was ours when we were in our proverbial cages is actually better and more real when we come to Christ. Psalm 119:114 says *He* is our hiding place. We can assume that God will provide us the safety we seek.

Corrie ten Boom sought a physical hiding place for oppressed people because she was exercising an eternal belief that God is our ultimate hiding place. She believed that because God provided safe refuge, she should provide physical refuge on His behalf. And that is how she fought for freedom.

Like Corrie ten Boom, we must fight for freedom all the time. We must fight for it for ourselves because we would want it for other people. You wouldn't want your best friend to be weighed down by sin or shame. You wouldn't want your mom to believe lies about herself. You'd want them to walk in beautiful freedom, and so you have to go there yourself. It's impossible to guide people into something you've never experienced.

Freedom is incredibly winsome because it's so countercultural. We all think freedom is a great idea in principle, and we are drawn to it when we see it. That's why it's such an important part of evangelism and discipleship. True freedom only comes through Christ, and when people see it in you, they will want it for themselves. They may not know what it is, but this hope and spark are undeniable.

In order to help other women move toward freedom, which sounds like a pretty amazing calling, we have to be free ourselves. We have to know that in our standing before God, we *are* free. And we need to be walking toward acting more freely every day.

The Cost of Freedom

I can only imagine the hurry and the crazy clamor when the Israelites got word that it was time to go. The tipping point had been reached, as it always does in times of release. The Egyptians had grown increasingly freaked out and burdened by the plagues inflicted on their land. At this point, they just wanted the Israelites to *go*: "The Egyptians were urgent with the people to send them out of the land in haste. For they said, 'We shall all be dead'" (Exodus 12:33 ESV).

Exodus records that six hundred thousand men left Egypt that day. The women and children would have multiplied that number many times over. The households emptied in such a rush that they hadn't even added yeast to their bread yet. But they grabbed their dough bowls and strapped them to their backs. It was a grab-and-run sort of situation.

It was the moment maybe you wonder about too: *What would I bring from my house if I had only a moment's notice?* I'd grab my phone (which also serves as my camera, my map, my Bible, and on and on), for sure. But what would I have to leave behind? If I wanted freedom right then, I'd have to leave behind anything I couldn't gather quickly and carry. At that point, the Israelites didn't know if they'd be coming back, so they may not have worried about grabbing precious things. Only the things they'd need for a few days away. I know when I'm packing for a weekend trip, I don't worry about the sentimental bits. But unbeknownst to them, the Israelites were indeed packing for the trip of a lifetime.

Although it appears to start suddenly, this song of freedom had been playing in the background for hundreds of years. The Israelites couldn't foresee that exact instant of release, and that's how it is most of the time, isn't it? We can begin to formulate the best kinds of plans—chart it all out; plot it in Excel; make to-do lists. However, freedom sometimes comes gradually and sometimes all at once.

Like Scripture, all of history and indeed our own lives are a sweeping composition. There are staccato beats of significance, swelling times when the pressure is building, and tipping points of climax that push everything to change. We rarely have foreknowledge of when that tipping point will come, but we can surely feel the pulse quickening in that direction.

I find that freedom is like this for me. I have to first be awakened to the need. I'll have the clanging moments when something big happens, when I realize how important the change coming really is. Then I'll have seasons where nothing is happening, per se, but I can feel the rushing current that is hard to deny. I can feel my tune starting to slowly change. My life will be moving along, but in the background I can feel the boil starting to roll. It's bubbling to the surface and starting to get noisy in my mind. It becomes difficult to think of much else, but no decisive moment or shift or change has happened yet. There is no release.

It's in these times that I challenge us to remember: He is the one who releases us. There will be no moment of change until He ordains it or allows it. He is sovereign and sits above human reason or human time. He is working through the ages, bringing things to fruition in His perfect timing. It may seem to us as though our lives are limited to our experience, but really, God often works through generations to grant freedom.

The Israelites had endured hundreds of years of captivity when they left Egypt. The years were like an orchestral piece, really. At the end of Joseph's colorful life, the Israelites were ushered into a new era. After enjoying times of great plenty and then suffering through times of great need, the Israelites became a threat. The Israelites grew in number and power, and Pharaoh didn't like it: "'Behold, the people of Israel are too many and too mighty for us. Come, let us deal shrewdly with them, lest they multiply, and, if war breaks out, they join our enemies and fight against us and escape from the land.' Therefore, they set taskmasters over them to afflict them with heavy burdens" (Exodus 1:9–11 ESV).

Even in the midst of the oppression, the Israelites continued to multiply. The music was swelling louder and louder. Pharaoh sensed the crescendo and called to the midwives to squelch this growth at the source. He ordered that all baby boys be killed. But this just began another movement in the greater whole set in motion by the Composer. God took what was intended to harm the Israelites—evil, oppression, the death of all their baby boys— and turned it to good by promoting a lowly, enslaved Israelite boy named Moses into the family of Pharaoh.

As we follow the rest of the story, we see short bursts of quickening action. Exodus 2:11 tells of a grown-up Moses witnessing the injustice of an Egyptian beating a Hebrew, one of Moses' own people. Moses lashes out at the Egyptian, kills him, and buries him in the sand. We know it's only a matter of time until this act catches up with Moses. And it does the very next day. Someone saw the crime, even though Moses thought the coast had been clear, and eventually Pharaoh found out. Pharaoh wanted Moses killed, even though Moses was his own adopted grandson.

Even so, God would find a way to use that criminal Moses. He was about to feel the pinch of a call from within a burning bush—the Lord appointing him to lead a whole group of people into freedom: "The cry of the people of Israel has come to me, and I have also seen the oppression with which the Egyptians oppress them. Come, I will send you to Pharaoh that you may bring my people, the children of Israel, out of Egypt" (Exodus 3:9–10 ESV).

Now, the moment of freedom hadn't yet come for the Israelites. But we don't call moments of spiritual importance a "burning bush" for no reason. This was a "gradually, then all at once" time for Moses. His life, his bondage, his experience were all notes leading to this point in God's composition.

The next chapters read like Moses' spiritual memoir—which it is, considering Moses was the one writing. It is the story of God calling him, confirming him, building him up, and bringing a companion, Aaron, to hold him up when he was weary or unsure. We see Moses go through times when he doubted himself.

Exodus 5 narrates a short story of great importance. It is a tiny song within a song. This piece about Moses' life and the history of Israel foreshadows many movements of freedom through history— the struggle of hearing the call, trying, failing, and trying again. At the beginning of the chapter, Moses and Aaron approach Pharaoh and ask for freedom. It is their first attempt, their first request, and their first moment before active freedom fighting. It ultimately only leads to more struggles for the Israelites.

Pharaoh retaliates because of the audacity of Moses and Aaron. He heaps more hardship on the slaves of Israel and increases their workloads. He attacks their character, calling them "lazy" (Exodus 5:17). He deepens their oppression and digs in his heels—telling them to "go and get your own straw wherever you can find it, but your work will not be reduced at all" (Exodus 5:11).

Moses and Aaron heard a call from the Lord, and God

confirmed it through signs and miracles. The people of Israel believed that God was leading Moses, but that faith was about to take a doubtful turn. When Pharaoh assassinated the character of the slaves, adding more hardship and making it impossible for the slaves to complete their jobs, people began to wonder if the pursuit of freedom was really worth it. They were questioning whether it might just be better to submit to captivity.

This happens sometimes when the cost of freedom seems particularly high. Many people may agree that, in theory, release is required, but theory doesn't compel loyalty or sacrifice. The only thing that compels the necessary sacrifice is the Lord Himself. Because of this pushback, even Moses was desperate for understanding.

God ignites freedom in our hearts and fans it to a flame to help us catch the vision. When you grow tired of waiting for some sort of circumstantial freedom, remember there is a freedom that no circumstances can touch, a freedom that is more powerful than all else—and that is *freedom from the fear of death*.

While we wait for our freedom, we must remember that Jesus is the prize. Jesus is always the prize. Whatever we learn here on earth, however we grow or do good, it is all to be more like Christ. When we wait, we have the particular gift of allowing the Holy Spirit to build in us the fruit of His Spirit. When you abide and wait, you are uniquely pliable because you are living in trust and fixing your eyes on what is unseen.

Exodus and Deuteronomy read like spiritual memoirs, as with Corrie ten Boom's *The Hiding Place*—stories of being called, growing, waiting, doubting, and being encouraged. Moses has to keep returning to God and being renewed in His call and being reminded that God is God. Like the people of Israel, we cannot prefer captivity, because it isn't God's best, and God's sweeping narrative keeps riding the waves of freedom.

As you journey toward lasting freedom, there are going to be times when you long for the days of captivity. You're going to be out navigating a new and unknown wilderness, and you'll feel a pull to go back to the old days. When you are tempted to focus on the hot shame you feel when you remember your past, just think of the fresh future before you. If you seek the smothering cover of your preferred sin of the past, just remember that God sees you as clean, and you can walk in freedom. Sin has no power over you, in Jesus' name. If you are afraid of the way ahead, remember that He is holding you, and He has led countless captives to freedom before you. If you listen, you will hear Him singing your freedom song—a song that ends with strong notes of assurance that God will bring His plans of freedom to fruition. He *will* complete the good work He has begun in you.

PRAYER

Lord, let us not resist the tide of Your bringing heaven down to earth. Let us not go back for the pittance that is captivity simply because it is easy or comfortable. Let us remain strong in Your strength, remembering that we're already free in You. We just have to learn what the song sounds like when You play it; we have to learn how to dance to Your beat; and we have to always remember Your story. You set us free when Your Son was condemned, and You do not desire us to be held under the burden of slavery ever again. This is Your will for us, Lord. Help us believe it and stand in it. Amen.

JESS'S RESPONSE

Yes! I'm so glad Hayley brought up Galatians 5:1. Through the writing of this book, God really called me to look harder at that verse. It's one I've spouted for years without truly understanding. It's for freedom that Christ has set us free. For me, the only way I could settle into the meaning of this verse was to list all the opposites of this truth that I was believing.

I know I've been set free, but I honestly thought a few of the following:

- *It's for my husband's good that I've been set free so I can serve him.*
- *It's for God's relief that I've been set free because He's so exasperated with my bondage.*
- *It's for my own productivity that I've been set free so I can finally get on with life and get myself together.*

None of these are true. It's for freedom that I've been set free. It's because God desires my freedom, and it brings Him glory. And pardon the phrase, but isn't that freeing?

ELEVEN // JESS

Spreading Like Wildfire

After I met Jesus in the fall of 1999, I couldn't get enough. Man, I loved Him so much. I wanted to come home from school and just read, read, read my Bible. My body felt more at ease when my hands were on it. My mind felt peaceful when I heard worship music playing. I loved to talk to Him. Waking up each morning and remembering He was still there, it was like waking up to the best dream ever. I was smitten. But I had a serious problem—more like a host of serious problems.

I had a closet full of alcohol and drugs and a purse stuffed with cigarettes—all things I felt tied to and in need of. I had a boyfriend who scoffed at my newfound Jesus and was fond of telling me what a miserable human I was, which, of course, kept me coming back to him, hoping he'd change his mind and approve of me. I wasn't awesome in school, so I didn't have that going for me, and now that I had my time divided between Bible reading and being rebellious, I was left with even less time to study. On top of that, I had parents who were understandably wary about my newfound commitment to Christ and the warring lifestyle they feared I was still living in.

On top of all of these things, I had something new—conviction. Until that point, I had no real inner moral compass. I could know that what I was doing was incredibly hurtful and wrong and still do it, hoping only that I didn't get caught. But when Christ caught my heart, that all changed, and it was like my soul birthed tiny little sensors of feeling everywhere. I felt convicted and busted all day.

197

But I didn't know how to stop because I didn't know how to let anyone in. I felt trapped under the weight of my sin, and I couldn't tell anyone all that I was wrestling with inside my heart. I didn't feel I could tell anyone the beautiful things God was doing in my heart either. I didn't have an outlet.

A few months in, I cracked and attempted suicide twice. The first time started as a halfhearted attempt that continued into a full-blown and, thankfully, fruitless attempt. The next day I was safe, but my heart issues were all still there, boiling under the surface, only to resurface later in a second attempt. By God's grace, I did not take my life, and the next day I decided not to try again for a while. Not because I felt hope or peace or thought it was going to get any better, but mostly because I was scared of trying and failing again.

It wasn't until I found myself in a community of women committed to holding each other up that I began to heal. Light flooded the dark places of my heart months later when God miraculously brought a group of girls to walk with me—Katie, Molly, Courtney, Emily, and Lauren. Beth was our youth group leader, and she was a dazzling, beautiful, confident woman who let us into her apartment and her life. I felt safe and spurred on by those girls. I didn't tell them all of my dark and scary secrets all at once, but the enemy lost so much square footage in my heart when I was with them. I spent less time doing the things of this world I had been chained to and more time dancing with them and talking to Jesus. I broke up with the boyfriend, cut ties with the friends I'd done rebellious things with, emptied my closet of the contraband, and felt incredibly brave and confident in being a Christian. Because I had my sweet little crew, I wasn't alone, and I had an outlet.

Ladies, we are calling for revival, and revival takes a crew. We are stomping our feet into the ground and throwing our hands in the air and saying, "Father, please come and revive a generation of women! Revive future generations of women! Help us live wild and free." And we know that revival starts up close and personal, with first letting God work in our hearts and letting the Holy Spirit stir up the fire in our veins. And revival continues when we let the redeeming work He is doing in our lives spill out through our mouths and actions.

I am absolutely willing to bet all I have on the belief that God is moving in your heart and in your life right now. I mean, real talk, I pray it's through this book. I pray He is using these words to stir up wild and wonderful truths and open doors in your spirit that have long been locked up or that you believed to be nonexistent. But I know that I know—He is moving somehow and in some way.

The question isn't whether God is moving in your heart and in your life; it has to do with what you're going to do about it. Are you going to lock it up and pretend like you don't hear the thumps of conviction or the thrill of hope? Are you going to respond and surrender, letting Him wring every last ounce of His glory from your days? Are you going to keep it private, or are you going to shout it from the rooftops?

If you haven't already, now's the time. Text a friend. Write it on social media. Tell your husband. Share it with your roommate. Ask some women from church to meet. God's revival spreads and your enemy grows weaker when you start to pass it on. The small act of obedience that calls for sharing your heart can have monumental, kingdom-impacting dividends. Take a moment right now to think about how you can share your heart with someone else. If you don't know what to share, ask God. If you don't know who to share it with, ask God. Remember that as wild and free women, we count on Him to talk to us, and we believe with our whole hearts that He will.

When I share my salvation story, I jokingly say I became a believer because my sister did. I say it lightly, but it's really true, and

I'm grateful. My older sister, Katie, became solely surrendered to Jesus during her freshman year in college. I was three years younger and entrapped in some of the darkest sin in my life. Despite my rebellion and my absolute lack of spiritual awareness, she shared her heart with me unabashedly and repeatedly—telling me the new truths of her faith until the joy in her heart was contagious. I can remember the exact moment I looked at her face and gave in. I told Jesus I wanted what she had and I'd do anything to get it.

It didn't stop there, though, with Katie. She has literally never stopped spurring me on, and in the sixteen years since that night, I feel like I've been chasing after her as she chases after Jesus. She essentially talked me into marrying my husband, having children, entering ministry, and every other good endeavor I've entered into willingly because she shared her passion for those things with me. The most beautiful part is that I don't think she ever made a conscious decision to make me her life's ministry. She has just let God's fire and revival take her on a wild ride and then told me about it the whole way.

Call Her Up Instead of Calling Her Out

Hayley was the first person I ever heard use the word *carefrontation*. When she unpacked the idea, I got that sick feeling in my stomach because I knew only too well what she was describing. "You know, carefrontation is when a friend or a woman in your church is calling you out about something. You know someone is disappointed in you—you're not sure what about—and they come alone or in a group to let you know what it is."

I've been on both sides of carefrontation. I've had the anxiety build in my stomach for weeks as I prepared to share my heart with a friend who had hurt me. I've blurted out my pain at the most inopportune moments, only to regret my cavalier discussion of relational hardship. I've also heard the sound of my heart beating loudly inside my ears as I read an email from a friend or acquaintance letting me know how I've let them down. Maybe you've never been carefronted, but I'm willing to bet that at some point in your life you've felt called out.

Not for a second do I want to seem like I'm not all for women speaking truth into one another's lives. I love to talk things out; I rarely avoid conflict; and my spiritual gifts include discernment. I believe in people sharpening people, just as iron sharpens iron, as Proverbs 27:17 tells us. I don't want to live in a Christian world where we don't feel like we have the liberty to be honest with one another and love each other through gentle, loving, and patient correction. That kind of culture does not feel wild or free to me—it feels stifled, prideful, and scared.

But I've learned something about speaking truth that feels like a healthy alternative and is less likely to leave women feeling deflated and dejected. Instead of calling women out, we should most often be calling them up.

First of all, I resonate with many Christian women today who are terrified of being found out. These are the frightened thoughts of women I know:

- *What if someone read all my text messages?*
- *What if someone knew what I was really thinking?*
- *What if my friends knew how I speak to my children when no one is around?*
- *Would people laugh at my dreams and ministry desires?*
- *Would I be allowed to serve in ministry if other women knew I'd had an abortion?*

- *What would happen if I posted a picture on Instagram with no filter? Or even worse, what if I posted what I ate for breakfast or what the floor of my bedroom looks like as I'm getting dressed for a date?*

We do not want to be found out. So why would any of us enjoy being called out?

The gospel levels the playing field in that it alleviates the need to hide our sin or brokenness. God didn't make a way for us to be made one with Him because He knew we had it all together; He made a way because He knew we were broken and would screw it all up. At the foot of the cross, we are all found out. We are all covered in the blood of Jesus. We are all made whole again. If you've been hiding or running away to avoid being confronted, I know it will be hard—but you can rest at His feet. He is not surprised by your sin or shocked by your humanity. And in community—in real, live, godly community—it should be the exact same.

Second, I don't believe any of us are qualified to call someone out if we're all on the same level of godliness and holiness. Since "there is now no condemnation" against you (Romans 8:1) and you've been made one with Christ Jesus, so have I. I cannot call you out, because I'm in the same mess you're in. But you and I? We can call each other up. We can point one another's eyes to Jesus. We can remind each other of our callings in the name of Christ our Lord. We can speak upward to one another, reminding each other that He who began a good work in us will be faithful to complete it. In the name of Jesus, we can call each other up.

Reminding one another that our struggle is not against flesh and blood but against the spiritual forces of evil, we can call each other up to the knowledge that no weapon forged against us can prevail. We can remind one another that it's for freedom that we've been set free. We can call one another to wild praise, to lift up our hands in prayer and worship, as the psalms tell us to do. We can proclaim Isaiah 61 over each other, admonishing one another to walk in freedom and to join God's mission to set the captives free.

It may be that calling one another up comes with a little gentle correction and a loving rebuke, but as wild and free women, we don't need to call each other out. We don't need to isolate our sisters in their sin. We need to remind them we're right there with them, put their eyes back on Jesus, and move forward together. And Lord help us if the only time other men and women hear us call them up is when we have a bone to pick with them. We *get* to call them up—we don't have to—and we get to call community up with us from the start of the day until the end of the night.

We get to call our kids up and remind them of the glorious inheritance they have in Christ. We get to call our friends up, pointing out their giftedness, speaking life and hope into their ministries. We get to call our spouses up, not looking at them with eyes that point out their failures, but with eyes that, like the eyes of their Father, see where they're going. Because we are wild and free women who speak *life*, the native language of our Father, we can walk away from calling out and being called out. We can call one another up.

Once we've shared our hearts, the wild and free truths that God is swirling up in us—the dreams He's birthing and the convictions He's bringing . . .

Once we've pulled back the veil and let people into our mess—our beautiful, redeemed, gospel-covered mess . . .

Once we've laid down the practice of attacking one another, pecking at each other's sins and assuming we must hide our faults or be eaten alive . . .

We're ready for a wild and free tidal wave.

Can you picture it? Can you visualize the replication of wild and free that will happen in communities? Can you imagine the women called up to their places in the army of God, ready to take on the world—not in fear or frustration but in the hope of the

204 // Wild and Free

revival of a nation? I pray that many of you can picture it because you already live it. But if it feels far-off or nearly impossible, I pray that you'd throw off the disbelief that hinders you and ask God for fresh eyes to see what He can do.

Wild and free is spreading. Revival is catching fire.

Get Ready on Purpose

As we gear up to get wild and free, the words of the apostle Paul in his letter to the Ephesians can be our guide:

> Finally, be strong in the Lord and in his mighty power. Put on the full armor of God, so that you can take your stand against the devil's schemes. For our struggle is not against flesh and blood, but against the rulers, against the authorities, against the powers of this dark world and against the spiritual forces of evil in the heavenly realms. Therefore put on the full armor of God, so that when the day of evil comes, you may be able to stand your ground, and after you have done everything, to stand. Stand firm then, with the belt of truth buckled around your waist, with the breastplate of righteousness in place, and with your feet fitted with the readiness that comes from the gospel of peace. In addition to all this, take up the shield of faith, with which you can extinguish all the flaming arrows of the evil one. Take the helmet of salvation and the sword of the Spirit, which is the word of God.
>
> And pray in the Spirit on all occasions with all kinds of prayers and requests. With this in mind, be alert and always keep on praying for all the Lord's people.
>
> *Ephesians 6:10–18*

Once we've established our own identity, seen some wild and free revival in our lives, and joined hands with the sisters around us, it's time to get ready to do battle. We're going to camp out in Ephesians 6:10–18, and as we unpack it, I want you to imagine your girlfriends and yourself waiting on the sidelines of battle—ready to wage war and free the rest of the women still held captive by small and scared or defensive and restless living. So you're there, hand in hand, on the same team—are you ready to do some kingdom work? Let's start at the beginning of the passage and see what God wants to tell us. We're going to abolish "too much" and "not enough" once and for all, amen?

Ephesians 6:10: Be strong in the Lord. There have been so many times when I've gotten caught up in the ideology of wild and free and forgotten that it's not really my idea. I've forgotten that it's not about what I can muster up or what I can live out. It's *God's* strength and *His* idea. This is good news, but let's ask for a dump truck of humility before moving forward. *Father, we don't want to be strong in our thoughts or actions; we want to be strong in You.*

Ephesians 6:12: Who are we standing against? Ladies, if we want to see wild and free spread like wildfire, this is one of the most important distinctions we're going to have to make. Who are we fighting against? I don't believe we're fighting against other women, generations that have come before us, our husbands, pastors, or any men who might not fully see things the way we do.

Probably one of the most damaging things we can do is take our passion and pick fights with earthly assailants. In my past, and I'm assuming in yours too, the enemy has used the words and actions of other humans—friends, family, and leaders—to keep me from living truly wild and free. But the enemy has also used *my* words and actions to do the same in the lives of other women. So let's fight the right enemy. The enemy of our souls. Let's also fight him with the right and full knowledge that he's already been defeated and has no dominion here. In Jesus' name.

Ephesians 6:13: When the day comes. I love this passage of Scripture that ultimately points to our larger battle in God's kingdom and is pertinent for our daily battles for freedom as well. I really wish you could read this book from cover to cover, close it, and walk away, spending the rest of your days feeling nothing but wild freedom, doing ministry with courage, laughing at the days to come, fighting for freedom—and wearing bold, red lipstick all the while. Shoot, I wish that was my life too. But the truth is, even more days are ahead that will require us to face evil. On those days, the Bible tells us to stand our ground. Let's be ready and aware that our fight has just begun.

Ephesians 6:14: Go back to truth. I know we've spent this entire book walking through truths, applying truths, uncovering truths—but we're going to have to keep going. To live a wild life of replication that sets fire to the freedom of other women, we're going to have to keep putting on truth. Not weekly or monthly, but daily and hourly. One woman, consistently armed with the truth of who she is in the Lord, is a game changer for the entire kingdom. Put that truth on first. Put that truth on often.

Ephesians 6:14: Apply the gospel and remember where your righteousness comes from. As if we needed the reminder that head knowledge cannot save us, we've got to guard our hearts. There's a reason it's called the "breastplate of righteousness." Knowing that the blood of Jesus covers us and makes us united with Him is the very thing that shields our tender hearts from believing lies. We can't just win with knowledge; we have the gospel to defend us.

Ephesians 6:15: Keep no baggage; be ready to go. It took me a long time to understand what this whole "ready feet" business meant until someone wiser unpacked it for me. You know the gospel of peace has transformed your life when you say "no more" to striving, to working for approval, and to dwelling on past hurts, pains, and problems. Once your head and your heart are free because the peace of Christ has permeated your spirit and your identity, your hands and feet will be free and ready to run.

My husband beautifully describes the readiness of the gospel of peace by pointing to someone at an airline ticket counter who has passport and ticket in hand. They're not searching frantically for their things, spilling drinks, or talking on their cell phones. They're ready to go. Let it be so for those of us who are headed out to minister to others.

Ephesians 6:16: Protected by our belief. Wild women who are set free to share aren't timidly or defensively protecting their faith from the world, but neither are they battering people over the head with it like a weapon. Their faith *is* their protection; it is their first line of defense against the enemy. The author of Hebrews tells us that faith is being certain of what we hope for, convinced of what we cannot see. As wild women, we've got to know specifically what those things are that we're hoping in. And thankfully, as wild women, we do not fear putting our specific and passionate hope in Christ alone.

Ephesians 6:17: We've got one great weapon. There's just no way around it. We're not going to see a wild and free revival of women without Scripture. There will never be enough chorus key changes, encores, or mic drops to replace what the Word of God can do to stir up our souls. Without the Word, there isn't a speaker or human leader compelling enough to lead us; there isn't a worthy enough cause that can unite us. But if we will all pick up the same weapon and point it at the enemy of our souls instead of at one another, we will run victoriously forward, come out unscathed, and see the generations after us radically changed by the power of God.

Ephesians 6:18: Don't leave the Spirit behind. When Jesus left earth, He promised things would go better for us, not because we could handle this mess on our own, but because He was leaving us with a better helper—the Holy Spirit. Ephesians 6 encourages us to pray continually in the Spirit, which actually commands two things. To pray in the Spirit, we're going to really have to *believe* in the Spirit and stop ignoring this beautiful part of the Trinity who works with us and for us daily and intercedes on our behalf to the Father. Secondly, we're going to have to get intimate with God. It won't be enough to just put on all of these godly attributes and try to win this war on our own. We're going to have to continually walk with Him. Talk to Him. Move forward with Him.

////

The good news is that if we want to see a revival happen where women pick up their wild and free identities and move forward to advance His kingdom, our Father can do it all on His own. He didn't need Hayley and me to write this book. He doesn't need any of us to share about it. He doesn't even really need us to obey. The better news is that instead of just doing it all in the snap of a finger, He has invited us into the process. He has invited us to the front lines. He's handed us all we need to move step by step by step and push the kingdom of darkness back as we grab hold of the kingdom of light and pull wild and free down from the heavens, dumping it into all of our hearts and lives.

This is not what He expects of us; this is what He allows to happen in and through us. And I'm wondering—can you see it? Can you take a few moments and picture what it would look like for the generations coming after you to be set free? Can you picture your moms and your sisters and your best friends, and certainly *yourself*, living free of the trappings, outside of the box you've always seen yourself in? Can you imagine your daughters, your nieces, your younger friends growing up without even knowing what those trappings are, much less feeling like a slave to them? Can you imagine the world they'd live in thirty, fifty, one hundred years from now? Transformed and changed by the gospel in ways we could never even dream up?

I can see it now—the wildfire. I can hear it in your voice. I can see it in your eyes. It is familiar and it is lovely and it is holy. It is Jesus. It is He, as mighty as ever in you—roaring and flickering and ready to consume all the pain and heartache you've ever known. The fire is there, ready to refine and burn off the brokenness that this world has layered on us. The wildfire of freedom is spreading, and thank God, none of us are too far gone to be found by it.

PRAYER

Father, will You fan the flames like only You can? Will You turn an idea, a feeling, into a passion and a roaring glow of women with hearts blazing for Your kingdom and Your desires? Will You use us however You see fit to love other women and help them as they run with You? We want only what You want, but we believe specifically and wholeheartedly that You want a wild and free revival to spread like wildfire among Your daughters. And we boldly and confidently ask You to do that like only You can.

We love You. Thank You, thank You.

HAYLEY'S RESPONSE

Jennifer and Jeanetta were the women in my life who gave me a soft place to land, even while I was still sorting out my newfound faith from my previous non-Christian life. Those months felt like I was picking apart my spirit with tweezers under a microscope.

I needed to examine every part to discern what was healthy and what was dead and needed to be excised.

I never, ever felt called out by Jennifer and Jeanetta; I only felt like they were cheering me on. They lived their own faith in such a compelling way that I was drawn to Jesus in them. They didn't have to point out that I was hanging out with the wrong people or making dumb choices; those things sorted themselves out once Jesus was in charge of my life.

That's not to say there isn't a place for noticing sin in other people, but the attitude should always be that you know Christ is mighty in them and the Holy Spirit is guiding them. There should be absolutely no condemnation, but full faith that God has the power to change any heart.

I took a long time studying accountability and how to grow together in community, and these words from the letter to the Hebrews stood out: "Let us consider how we may spur one another on toward love and good deeds . . ." (Hebrews 10:24). Spurring one another on toward love and good works sounds exactly like what modern-day accountability hopes to achieve, and in the next verse, we see the "how" of the equation: "encouraging one another—and all the more as you see the Day approaching" (10:25).

A Campfire Commissioning

I love nothing more than sitting around a campfire with a bunch of friends on a warm summer night. I love the moments when day mingles with dusk and the air seems to have an electric hum. I love the crackle of the fire and the way the light plays off the features of the people I love. Something about firelight makes people look so beautiful. Those moments are ones I always try to trap in my memory. All my senses feel like I'm in a movie.

I close my eyes and try hard to imagine the joy Harriet Tubman must have felt when she crossed into a free state for the first time. Tubman had been a slave her entire life, born to a woman who was owned. The law stood: Every child born to a woman in bondage was automatically, at the moment of her birth, in bondage too. Isn't that the cruelest reality? Just like in Scripture, when we are enslaved, we pass down that bondage to our children as well.

After years of slavery, the thought of what might happen if she continued in bondage became too grave, and Harriet made a move toward freedom. Have you ever felt that way? Have you ever had a moment when you realized it was a far greater risk to remain where you were than to set off on a new path? We have to feel the distinct pain of our own enslavement before we'll find the courage to leave it for freedom. No one can force freedom on us; we must be active participants in our emancipation. As research professor Brené Brown says, "Hope is a function of struggle."[11]

I've lived to that point where I struggled against something so hard that I had no choice but to hope. I hoped for more than the defensive living I was doing. I'd long lived in a tightly closed bud. I was living small and scared, afraid to take up too much space in the world. I was hesitant to use my voice, terrified it would get me in trouble. I was spinning my wheels in an effort for approval and affection, and it was exhausting. To paraphrase the ubiquitous Anais Nin quote, my self-imposed defenses grew more uncomfortable until my discomfort finally outpaced my need for security. But I also felt that to bloom would be painful and difficult. I knew that being a full-blown flower was going to draw more attention and, as a by-product, more criticism. I knew a bud was safe, its outer leaves protecting the delicate insides like a shield. And I wanted to stay there—closed and small. But Psalm 28:7 tells us, "The LORD is my strength and my shield." If I really believed that God is my shield, I could take the risk and open up, believing that He would protect me. I could make myself vulnerable, even though it meant leaving behind the small cage I called home.

Because the threat to Harriet Tubman was very real, she couldn't stand to wait any longer. "There was one of two things I had a right to," she explained later. "Liberty or death; if I could not have one, I would have the other."[12] She left the struggle she knew intimately and set off on a dangerous move toward freedom. She moved by the light of the stars, night after night, until she crossed the state line into Pennsylvania, a free state. Later in her life, she recounted that moment when she went from being in bondage to living in freedom: "When I found I had crossed that line, I looked at my hands to see if I was the same person. There was such a glory over everything; the sun came like gold through the trees, and over the fields, and I felt like I was in heaven."[13]

To reach Philadelphia, her point of freedom, she utilized a vast system of safe houses and shrouded routes. You may remember learning about this path to freedom in grade school, the famous and fabled Underground Railroad.

I have long been fascinated by the Underground Railroad. In a day when long-distance communication was difficult, when the country was divided and on the brink of war, when there was no electricity, little medical care, and rudimentary roads, the Underground Railroad was a complex and sophisticated system. However, it's entirely different to be entertained by the story of the Underground Railroad than to be inspired by the reality of its existence. The Underground Railroad needed to exist to usher a mass of people from slavery to freedom. They needed secret hideouts and stops for rest along the way. The Underground Railroad was a very real need born out of a very real problem. It was orchestrated by impassioned individuals who risked their lives to personally achieve freedom and help others find freedom as well.

As "passengers" on the Underground Railroad, the escaped slaves would usually wait until nightfall and leave their safe haven under the heavy blanket of darkness. The smaller the moon, the better, because even its dim glint could reveal them to bounty hunters and law enforcement officers. Silently, they advanced through backwoods and marshlands toward the next station. For some, this mission to freedom proved more frightening than the idea of remaining enslaved. At least as a slave, you have an idea of what to expect tonight and tomorrow. When you leave the relative safety of your master, you enter an unknown wilderness. You are vulnerable; you don't know the traps to avoid; you face a whole new set of challenges.

Our own roads to freedom need to be built. It's high time we forge deeper intimacy with the Lord, believing all the things He says about Himself and us. We can understand our past, the unique ways we're trapped, and the patterns that got us to this point. We need most of all to identify what we're heading away from. We need to know the value of leaving it behind.

It's not an easy job, but it's one you're equipped for. You're even commissioned to do it. Galatians 5:13 reads, "You, my brothers and sisters, were called to be free." He expects you to live freely. He has given you that job. It's time to step up and take on the task at hand.

If you don't have the courage, ask God for it. If you don't know how to make a freedom trail, ask Him. If you wonder why it's worth it, by all means, beg Him to show you. If you aren't convinced that you should leave and can leave, you'll never make it to lasting freedom.

But with God, anything is possible. He can turn systems of oppression upside down. He can turn abusers into advocates. He can turn victims into healers.

Go on and follow your Father to freedom. Maybe He's even placed a sister along the path to guide you. Once you've seen the glory of freedom, make sure to go back and be an outpost for others. Be a station where they can stop and rest. Love and serve them and point the way. Not one single person is in unreachable bondage with the power of Christ. He has made a way for us all.

Freedom for One Is Not Enough

It's massively important to remember that all things are possible with God. When I get discouraged and things feel too big and I feel too small, I just utter that verse (Matthew 19:26) over and over and over. I also repeat Philippians 4:13 (NKJV): "I can do all things through Christ who strengthens me." These two verses remind me that even the toughest challenges do not faze God.

Once we find freedom for ourselves, it compels us to seek it for others. There is something so sweet about living freely. It's seeing how God's love compels us to love and God's grace compels us to forgive. God's freedom for us compels us to help others get to freedom too.

Harriet Tubman did not sit around and get comfortable in her newfound freedom, doing as she pleased and looking after her own interests. Instead, she utilized her freedom to travel back, gather other willing slaves, and bring them to that place where the sun was gold and there was so much glory it felt like heaven. Having been enslaved and then tasting freedom, she couldn't rightly celebrate her own freedom without feeling the bondage burden of her loved ones.

She became a charismatic and magnetic woman who rescued men and women from the chains of slavery and led them to lives of freedom. People trusted her because it was so obvious that she had tasted freedom. She was a woman on a mission.

And when you've tasted freedom? When you've walked away from defensive living, you can say good-bye to the heaviness of others' expectations. You can walk without crippling insecurity. You can live with your imperfect self, knowing that you're covered in Christ.

When you've seen the golden, glittering glory, you'll want others to live in that place too. It won't be enough to live there on your own; you'll ache to see your friends and sisters and mother living in freedom with you. It will pain you to see others still in shackles to their masters.

But those in chains can rarely free themselves. They need someone to enter in, give them permission to leave, and then usher them to safety. We need someone who has walked the road before us and can show us the way, providing a measure of safety along the treacherous path. We need someone to tell us what glory looks like and feels like. And only a person who has tasted freedom can describe its sweet abundance.

I know that abundance, and I know how I yearn for someone I love to rise up and seize their freedom and run. I have wanted to hug someone so long that they know they are valued. I know what it is like to taste freedom and turn around to bring others to the source. That desire is good, and it is from the source Himself, God our Father. He longs for us to walk in freedom with Him, mastered by no other person or thing. I have tasted freedom, and I have lived freely. It is sweet, and it is good.

Do you think that freedom is so good and so worth having that you'd risk your very life to see others set free? In all of Scripture, we see that the promise of heaven and of God's presence is so wonderful that it should compel us to rescue others. This is the Great Commission laid out for believers in Matthew 28. People who have come to know the goodness of God should not keep that good news to themselves. We are told to go and make disciples, leading them to eternal freedom in Christ.

That is the commissioning for each of us. I wish you were at my campfire so I could look you straight in the face and you could see the sparkle in my eyes when I get worked up about living freely. I would tell you how much your Father loves you. I would tell you He made you good because He is wholly good. I would tell you how beautiful you are when you're living wildly for His glory. I would whisper how great freedom is, ask if you've tasted it, and then challenge you to share it. I'd commission you to go find your friends and help them on the path to freedom.

In America, it is rare to have to risk our lives for the spiritual freedom of others, but we may have to risk other things that are important to us. Because corrupt social systems are threatened when people live freely, you will often find that people will resist your freedom. I have found, especially in some spiritual circles, that women who are living in the freedom of Christ will some-times raise eyebrows. Their motives or righteousness may be called into question, and it may appear they are making a scene or not playing by the rules. *This is essentially the same old lie that women are either too much or not enough.* Throw off that business, because it simply isn't true.

A New Kind of Freedom Fighter

In American culture, we often equate freedom with doing what-ever we want and getting whatever we please. Living freely means having no boundaries or restrictions. We all know women who believe this to be true and who behave accordingly. They are often brash, abrasive, unloving, unwise, discontent, and agitated. It almost seems that they are beholden to another master, which is themselves. This isn't the case in a Christian's life at all. Our bond to Christ is indelible and eternal; God's Word and the Holy Spirit inform our actions and decisions. Selfishly driven autonomy feels empowering for a time, but it is a counterfeit of true freedom.

A free woman isn't untethered and out of control; she is rooted in God and submitted to His control. We want to label her, to find a place to categorize her in our minds, but no label fits. Her freedom, her ease in herself, her purpose and joy—they all come from being secure in her identity in Christ.

Have you ever been around a woman who was truly free? She was secure in her identity, not because she was beautiful; even beautiful women have insecurities. She was secure, not because she was brilliant; even brilliant women don't know everything. She was secure, not because she was successful; even successful women have failures. Her security didn't depend on excelling or pleasing.

That freedom she possessed? She was free because her master

was the King of the land, and He had set her free. He had said she should be mastered by no other thing. When a woman knows she is completely and utterly free, she doesn't fear the opinions of others, doesn't fear failing, and doesn't stay up late worrying about the details. She walks through her days knowing she is free indeed. She is like the storied woman of Proverbs 31, who throws her head back and laughs at the days of her future.

The women who can have cheerful peace about the future are the most attractive kinds of women. Women who daily walk in freedom are so magnetic because everyone wants even the smallest taste of freedom. There is something palpably different about the way they carry themselves, about the spark in their eye, and about their boldness. They may have different personalities—quiet or boisterous, natural leaders or gifted servants—but the spirit of freedom shines through them all the same.

Let me tell you about the women in my life who have led me in my path of freedom. They were like conductors on the Underground Railroad, blazing a trail and shining the light for all to see.

Truth Telling

I blinked back tears as I picked an errant thread from the cuff of my sweatshirt. I felt so seen and known, and because of that, I felt very exposed. If there's one thing that makes me squirm more than anything, it's the feeling of being exposed, even if it's for good reason.

A woman who had invested in me was pointing out some relationships she had observed in my life. She wanted to know if I was being vulnerable in those friendships—was I allowing myself to be known? Or out of fear of being hurt or misunderstood, had I shrunk back and played it safe?

This is the kind of woman you want in your life. She makes

me nervous in the best ways. I feel spurred on and a little off-kilter every time I leave a conversation with her. She calls things as she sees them, but she exudes so much peace in her own life that you feel compelled to listen. It's not always easy because what she has to say is often pointed and uncomfortable. She has fought hard for peace, freedom, and courage in her own life, and she pushes hard for it in my life too.

I was watching her live it out, and even from far away it was beautiful. I practically begged her for her time, just to speak wisdom into my life. She gifts me with these little wisdom-packed conversations where she just goes right to the core of things. She doesn't beat around the bush, although she's the sweetest and kindest woman I've ever known. She's disarming because she's kind of kooky like me. But I am never fooled. She knows the Lord and believes Him at His Word. She walks hand in hand with Him every single day and knows that He is her only hope.

The hard part is, when you meet a woman like her, she doesn't allow you to stay chained to unhealthy behaviors or beliefs. It's uncomfortable. But she feels the goodness of freedom and doesn't want to mess around with the piddly lies of captivity. She knows what a boxed-up life looks like, and she knows she's never going back, and she'll be darned if she's going to see her friends live there either.

She spoke into parts of my life that everyone else praised. She saw through the good-girl behaviors to the heart of the issue: I was performing all the time for approval. She saw the potential pitfalls of some lies I was believing. She knows there are certain kinds of bondage the world applauds. There is hardly a worse kind of captivity than the captivity everyone says you should feel grateful for.

She urges me to a slower pace when the rest of the world seems to love the culture of more and now. She tells me that God just wants my heart, even when big and public works are what the world calls us to. She presses in when I would rather go it alone. She is brave and gets in my business a little, even when our culture tells us to mind our own. She speaks the language of small, abiding, and faithful. It sounds an awful lot like the voice of the Father.

This is the kind of woman I want to be.

I learned from that free woman what it's like to press in on someone's life. It's nerve-racking for me because I desperately want to give people their space. After all, I *love* my own space. I like my privacy; I don't love to cuddle; and I prefer a nice handshake to a hug. I know, I'm weird. All of this keeps me from asking the hard questions and often getting to the heart of the matter.

But because of her, I know that nothing is more freeing than being in the presence of another woman who has been set free. She will ask you questions, love you regardless of the answer, and spur you on to more intimacy with the Lord.

Americans (privacy junkies like me) are often caught completely off guard by this brand of living. This kind of honesty and intimacy is foreign in our culture, but it's also deeply alluring. We long to be seen and known, and we're desperately missing it in our female relationships. We stay out of each other's junk, because if we butt in, we're exposing ourselves too.

Because it is so attractive, this kind of freedom and intimacy is effective in both evangelism and discipleship. When I think back to what first intrigued me about the whole Jesus thing, it was the complete and genuine interest a few key believers took in my life. It was the truth they spoke to me and how unguarded they were in their own lives. We have a holy responsibility to examine the ways we've been chained and then gloriously freed in order to love and lead the next generation of women well.

Tethered to Each Other

I had two women in high school who poured countless hours into me, even when I was a crazy fifteen-year-old who was making really poor decisions. My parents were in the throes of post-divorce, and in their preoccupation, I felt massively unseen in my life. But these women saw me. They invited me into their worlds, and I witnessed an untethered joy I'd never really seen before. They asked me questions, gave me opinions, and took interest in the things that made me a unique creation.

These women were the first truth tellers who helped cut the strings holding me to the lie that I had it all figured out and could save myself. They beautifully lived out the responsibility we have to each other to walk in freedom. Because they were free, I believed for the first time that there was something more out there than I had ever tasted.

I went to a little Midwestern Christian college where students really loved the Lord, but an immense amount of rules and playing nice was involved. I bought into it with the vigor and excitement of a freshly minted Christian college girl. I wanted to grow spiritually; I wanted community; and I wanted a real and alive faith.

There was a girl who lived across the hall who was the wildest and freest girl I'd ever met. She believed there must be more to God than what we were living out. She hoped and believed there was so much more power than just following rules and appearing good. She gathered ten of the wildest women she knew for a yearlong mentorship and fellowship community. She expected our commitment to growth and freedom.

After college, I was surrounded by a community of women who were free in Christ. It was in this church family that I was lucky enough to grow as a woman. My second time to cross the threshold of that building, I was hugely pregnant and was balancing a bowl of cranberry pecan salad on my big belly—my contribution to a women's ministry potluck. I didn't know a soul, and I didn't particularly know why I was there, other than I'd melt from idleness if I stayed alone in our apartment another evening. I had only attended the church one Sunday, alone, because my husband was out of town for work again. This drop-in was out of character for me, but I was emboldened by the fact that no one in the state of North Carolina knew I existed.

I remained with that group of women for the next four years. It was at that church with the concrete floors and enormous fireplace that I realized my relationship with God wasn't about doing cartwheels for His approval. I didn't have to check off the boxes of a job well done, hoping to ace my midterm faith exam. Spiritual disciplines, rather than tedious, became Spirit-led, and I gladly obeyed.

I had my first babies in that church body, and those women and men cared for us and ushered me into the foreign season of new motherhood. If there is a season at all when a woman needs to be told she is lovely and free, it is when she is stuck in a tiny apartment, in a body that feels unreal, aching with pride for her newborn child. Constantly hearing the drumbeat of the gospel and the song of freedom during that brand-new time taught me that it was normal and expected that I live freely. I found merciful and gracious purpose in that time, when most of my days were spent laboring over diapers and bottles. I invested in that body of women, and as they led me into freedom, I led others in the same direction.

I believe those women who fought for my spiritual liberty in that particular season changed the trajectory of my life as a Christian woman. I learned that love was not directly tied to performance, that trust wasn't born out of control, and that God was not impressed by my showing off. I continued falling short of perfection, as I do today, but I learned to abide—through prayer, through community, and through showing up every week and welcoming vulnerability by being vulnerable myself.

Because You Are Free

It's time to change your language and your behavior; it's time to act like the free woman you are. You'll be faced with a decision. Will you believe God has made you free? Do you believe strongly enough to walk into freedom? Your adventure does not end when you reach freedom. Will you enter back into the messiness of life and encourage others toward freedom? You won't be going alone, so don't be afraid. The very Spirit of God will compel you, guide you, and provide what you'll need for each leg of the journey. All you need to get started is the willingness to be vulnerable, obedient, and brave.

Living your life freely is an inspiration to everyone around you. It is refreshing to come across a woman who speaks her native language of life because she knows she cannot possibly outgive the Giver or outlove the Lover. It is life-changing to come into contact with someone who sees you and all your flaws, loves you, and challenges you to love yourself and the God who created you.

In any movement of freedom, there is a spark from the Holy Spirit that has the gold and glittering glint of glory. There is that first moment in the life of a community where flint yields flame and a fire begins to smolder. We must vulnerably yield to the spark, obediently fan the flame, and bravely allow the smolder.

In my wildest hope, we will begin to see more communities of women free and unashamed. They will walk away from the shame and bondage of their past and live in wild freedom today. Their hope will be secure, and they won't have to worry. They will be living and breathing inspiration for other women to walk toward the golden glory of freedom.

The free women in these communities will hold the hand of a friend—someone they love who is still enslaved to something, maybe image issues or shame or abuse. They'll walk hand in hand. They'll be stronger together, and when they grow faint, they can sit in each other's company. Those friends can navigate the dark roads, warning each other of the dips in the terrain and the threats in the distance, always pointing toward freedom.

The woman who is free will constantly remind the others that freedom is worth it. She sees further down the road and knows that the discomfort of leaving captivity is a small price to pay for the value of entering freedom. She opens herself up, putting down her shield and showing other women when it is safe to do the same. It's nearly impossible for community to thrive in vulnerability until someone takes the massively risky first step of lowering their guard.

Don't be fooled. The walk to freedom is terrifying. It is full of danger, risk, and vulnerability. You can't carry your cage with you to freedom. You have to open the door, walk out, and leave that cage behind. You have to abandon the life of captivity you know so well. You may know your cage so intimately that it feels comforting, like home to you. And it's hard to leave home for some supposedly better thing. But God has promised something much better.

Harriet Tubman knew that freedom was better than captivity. She also knew that freedom was not only for her but also for everyone. On Harriet's first attempt at freedom, she compelled her brothers to join her. They were young men at the time, able-bodied for the trek. Harriet led the way, and her brothers followed, but they soon decided to turn around, meaning Harriet was also forced to return.

Harriet left again shortly thereafter—this time without her brothers—but it's likely she never forgot losing her brothers back to the captivity they'd always known. When she began leading others north to freedom the following year, she made it abundantly clear to those who requested to go with her that turning back was not an option. Years later, as she reflected on her eight years as conductor of the Underground Railroad, she was able to say what most conductors couldn't say: "I never ran my train off the track . . . and I never lost a passenger."[14]

As we walk toward freedom, those who walk with us may grow weary and scared. There are some who will turn back, not ready to grab hold of the hope we've all been given but cannot always see. There may be times when we grow so tired and lonesome that we are tempted to slide back into captivity ourselves.

But keep on. Keep your eyes up. Look to the North Star and take hold of the freedom that is rightfully yours. Be the one who dares to sing out loud a spiritual song of liberty, comforting and guiding others out of the darkness. Be one of the brave and willing few who cries out for freedom and walks with others who ache for it too. Stand up and live out these words of the apostle Paul: "Brothers and sisters, I do not consider myself yet to have taken hold of it. But one thing I do: Forgetting what is behind and straining toward what is ahead, I press on toward the goal to win the prize for which God has called me heavenward in Christ Jesus" (Philippians 3:13–14).

Leading Others to Freedom

Because freed-up women are so rare and attractive, they often become excellent evangelists and disciple makers. In this day and age (and it's true throughout history), women are desperate for freedom. Everyone wants to know a free woman's secret. The secret is Jesus. Because He has set us free, He has equipped us to lead others to freedom as well. Harriet Tubman could never have led others to freedom had she not first walked the Underground Railroad herself. But because she had, other slaves trusted her to lead the way. They trusted her with their very lives because of her testimony of freedom. Being able to testify to your own freedom in Christ can be the most compelling story you can tell. Because we are all naturally drawn to some kind of master (the same way the people of the Old Testament were drawn to worshiping idols), everyone can relate to feeling entrapped or ensnared.

As a little girl, I remember aching to fall asleep because I was so ensnared by anxiety. My head physically hurt from the thoughts tumbling through my mind. I would replay my day, remembering people's reactions to things I said, remembering how I'd embarrassed myself, and mostly remembering what I'd done wrong. I was steeped in hot shame, and I was so young that I didn't even know what shame was. I think I was about seven or eight, and I couldn't fall asleep without talk radio playing on my square, white digital alarm clock. The voices of men and women debating issues occupied my mind better than soft rock, and without something actively holding my attention, my thoughts would return to the gauntlet of worry and anxiety.

One of my sons has a predilection toward worry, and I hate that he comes by it honestly. I pray about this inclination of his all the time, praying that I will lead well and that God will spare him the anxiety I've battled my entire life. I pray that God will break the generational predisposition to the sin of worry. One night recently, my son had a hard time sleeping. When I walked into his room, I felt like I was walking into my childhood bedroom. I don't know how else to describe it, but worry hung thick in the air. I maneuvered around the Legos that littered my path, a figurative land mine in the dark. I went up on the tips of my toes and peeked through the slats of his bunk bed, disoriented by the dark and the height. My eyes searched for my boy under all those heavy covers, and I found him still and small and scared.

In that moment, something moved in my soul. I felt eternity shift, and I know the Holy Spirit gave me an urgency I'd never experienced. I draped my hand awkwardly over the top bunk rail and onto my son's back, and I asked him to sit up. I wanted to look him square in the face and know that he heard me. I grabbed his hands and went on to tell him about my square, white talk-radio-playing alarm clock. I told him how when I was a little girl, I never felt peace and was always worried. I spoke lower and softer, telling him how my childhood mind was never settled and how sad I felt right in that moment in his room for little me. I desperately did not want my son to experience those lonely, obsessive, nervous nights. I told him I hoped that one day he would know Jesus, because Jesus is peace. At this point, my eyes were making his sheets wet with slow, hot, drip-dropping tears. I explained that because my mom and dad didn't know Jesus, I never knew anyone who could be comfort and peace like Jesus is. I whispered how much I desired peace for him and how Jesus could take his worry away. It was the first time I had made myself intimately vulnerable to my son for the sake of the gospel and for his freedom. It was aching, and it was terrifying, and it was good.

My eyes still prick with stinging tears when I think back to that night. I spoke freedom over my son, and I said the words I wish I could say to my smaller self. I said the words and offered the hope I wish someone had soothed me with as a child. Even as I heard the words escape my own mouth, that promise of the peace of Jesus felt like a balm. It was healing to walk out of that painful memory so I could lead my son differently. Living freely allows us to operate out of the truth we know about God rather than the memory, worry, or wounds of our past.

Being able to express that the key to your freedom is Jesus makes you winsome for the gospel. The secrets people hold tightly are snares that bind them and hold them hostage, often for life. When someone keeps those masters in the dark, shame can bloom and freedom be stifled. But by now we know that if we endure the terrifying journey to freedom, which requires vulnerability, bravery, and obedience, we will be free indeed.

Now I have the words to say to someone in bondage, even my little-girl, talk-radio-loving self. I can shake those chains to let her know they're there. I can soothe her and tell her of my own past chains. I can paint a dozen pictures from my own life when I decided to leave the cage and pursue true and wild freedom. I can hold her hand and keep her company on the journey away from bondage.

Circle 'Round the Fire

Let me hold your hand—oh, how I wish I could! Imagine we're sitting under quilts worn with age and stories. Imagine the air is crisp, and the fire blinks and wisps. The night has grown chilly as the sun has said good night and tucked itself in. All our friends were talking to each other, but it's suddenly gotten quiet. It's that moment when it feels like something important is hanging in the air.

And because I'm never short on words, I'm going to take a moment to get a little mouthy. I need you to know, because this is important.

Go ahead—let's all join hands around this fire. Now listen.

The freest women I know are elderly. They've thrown off every earthly trapping and are as close to God as a newborn baby. They've gone from fresh-faced to wise to seasoned, and they are now trading earthly abilities for heavenly gain. They're light as a feather because there are just so few things holding them back.

I love the women I know who have hair so white it looks like a halo, but let's not wait until we're their age to feel wild and free. Think of how we'd regret it if we looked back at pictures of ourselves when we were young and wondered why we felt so weighed down. We already *are* wild and free, right here and right now in Jesus. It's just like salvation; we have to claim it and then walk forward.

Let's decide that *now* is the time. Tonight is the night we'll know we're wild and free. We are wild when we're walking in who God created us to be. You can do that, yeah? You know you were made good, because God Himself is good and therefore can create only good things. I believe that to be true.

And sweet girl, I hear you. I can hear the thoughts creeping up on you. But so much has happened since then. I know. The world is broken and hurting, and it is sometimes very scary indeed. But He is good. And He has already overcome.

If we are to walk freely, then we have to rest in what Jesus has already done for us. It has little to do with us and everything to do with Him. Doesn't that take the weight off? Can you imagine everything that has held you back from wild freedom just floating up like the cracking plumes of fire? Can you let them go and say farewell?

It's time, because you've been called. You are among a royal and holy group, set apart for the glory of the Lord. It's time to walk away from here changed. Find your sisters, grab their hands, and speak life to each other. When your girl forgets, remind her. When she stumbles, grab her arm so she doesn't skin her knee. If she falls straight down and feels the burn of injury, encourage her and carry her to the Healer. This isn't a journey for the faint of heart. It's not a path to travel alone.

As you begin the dark walk toward wild freedom, hand in hand with your soul sisters, when you are afraid that with any misstep or snap of a twig you'll be jettisoned back to bondage, remember: Where you are going is golden and good. It is close to glory because it is close to the heart of God. Freedom is beautiful, and it's a foretaste of heaven. Keep that thought in your mind as you move, however slowly, however carefully, toward the land of wild freedom.

Sing with me this anthem of *Wild and Free* as we take the first step in this incredible journey:

> *The world may tell us we're too much and never enough.*
> *But we can walk wildly in who God created us to be*
> *and rest freely in the work Jesus did for us.*
> *We do not have to be confined or conformed by cultural*
>   *expectations.*
> *We are unchained from our past and unafraid of our future.*
> *We choose compassion over comparison.*
> *We love without condition, without reserve.*
> *Our eyes are on God; we hold nothing back;*
> *we run fast and strong; we do not hide our light.*
> *We aren't wild and free for our sake alone;*
> *rather we sing life, hope, and truth over the world*
> *with abandon—just as our God sings over us.*
> *We are wild and free.*
> *And we are poised to do mighty things, in Christ alone.*

PRAYER

Heavenly Father, as You release us, will You compel us to go after our sisters and friends? Will You compel us to remain in freedom so we can live it out for our daughters, breaking the ties that bind us in sin generationally? Will You please give us the strength, through Your power, to be women who fight for the freedom of others?

Freedom is only from You, Lord. It is only on Your time. But we know that You can do things in an instant, and we pray that You'd set off a tidal wave of freedom that crashes onto the shores of every continent. Lord, give us today our daily bread. Give us the taste we need to hunger for freedom in areas of our lives we didn't know were still in bondage.

You, Father, are freedom. You are the wild, lavish, and unhindered God who has seen and chosen us as daughters. We're grateful for Your grace and release, God. Amen.

Acknowledgments

Jess thanks:

Nick, I'm not sure you knew exactly what you were getting into when you married this wild woman—but you have loved me relentlessly regardless. Your quiet strength, grace, and leadership have given me space to start growing into the woman God made me to be. Thank you isn't enough.

Mama, you're my matriarch of *Wild and Free*. You were serving cheese and crackers long before we called it charcuterie, starting businesses and ministries when there weren't networks or websites, and loving well when it wasn't easy. That big red ring brought me back to life.

Ruby dear, there's still no one I know who lives these words better than you. I know Jesus because I saw Him on your face and wanted what you have, and the same goes for any other fun, worshipful, or redeemed part of my life. #mysame

Caroline, what an inheritance we have in Jesus *and* in our family! Here's to a sweet future of sisterhood and life and loving alongside one another.

Brittany, Ruth had nothing on you. You have been God's gift to me in so many ways. Laughter, processing, encouragement, correction, cookies, foot fights, tears, and more laughter.

Rach Kincaid, Sarah Jacobs, Laura Troutman, Meredith Schauer, Stephanie Snell, Karen Yim, and, last but absolutely not least, Lara Casey: Thank you for praying these words out and holding up my arms!

Jacey, Jen, and Alicia: Thank you for letting me process and pace around our office with my arms waving wildly. Thanks for letting me learn how to lead with you.

Thank you so much to the ladies who've encouraged me in this calling that doesn't really have a description or boundaries. You have been my commissioning in one way or another: Jessica Honegger, Jennie Allen, Debbie Wickwire, and Jess Wolstenholm.

To the ladies of Gospel Community Charleston: You're the ones I want to live wild and free with the most.

Last but certainly not least—Elias, Glory, Benja, and Cannon: Thanks for loving me as God guides me through motherhood and womanhood and all of our life experiences. Boys, I pray for your future wild women every day of my life. Gloriana, the enemy shudders at how mighty God is in you. You are the best.

Hayley thanks:

Mike, you've always been up for my wild-eyed ideas, and you've cheered me on so well. Your love has been the most tangible, constant human grace in my life. Without it I surely wouldn't know the Lord as well. Thanks for flipping a coin and jumping in with both feet. We're sure on an adventure, my love.

Mom, Grammers, and Grandma, I love seeing the ways you're gifted, and I love learning from you. As I've gotten older, I only appreciate you more.

Dad and Grandpa, thank you for teaching me I was strong and smart. You taught me about presidents and the stock market. Because of you, I never felt like being a girl was a hindrance.

Kevin and Robin, the grandparents Morgan and the grandparents Gates, thank you for loving me like your own. I feel woven into your spiritual heritage, and that's an unearned gift from God.

Myquillyn Smith, Lara Casey, and Susie Davis: Thank you for the ways you've encouraged me and challenged me in this crazy job I never dreamed of having. Giving life to words is surely one of the wildest things ever.

Jill and Jenny, you've been my great friends for a long time. Glad our families get to grow up together. Love you both.

Sara, the way you love people is extravagant. You were the best gift God could have given me—and right in my backyard!

Whitney, Lindsey, Brittany, Kelly, and Tara: You girls were just what I needed.

Annie: Love you, sweet girl.

Now, my boys. The four of you are my wild. There is no greater privilege than loving you well.

- Noah Preston, I pray that you grow big and strong and become a man who chases after God with all your heart.
- Cooper James, I pray that you grow to be a man of conviction and compassion who knows and loves the Lord intimately.
- Asher Brax, I pray that when you speak hard truth, people hear only grace and love.
- Eli Patrick, I pray that you love and follow God in wild and imaginative ways.

I've been captivated by each of you from the moment I heard your galloping little heartbeats. I love you, my wild boys.

Together, we thank:

Jenni Burke, since you were our top-pick agent and also our spiritual fleece for whether or not we should write this book, you'll never know how grateful we are for that day in May when you told us you believed in *Wild and Free* and in us. Thank you for holding our hands and telling us when to put our lipstick on. We love you!

Stephanie Smith, we knew the moment we met with you that you were the absolute best possible option to carry this book to fruition. Thanks for handling our book baby with so much love and care, for making it better than it could've ever been without you. *You* are wild and free, and we cannot thank you enough.

To the entire team at Zondervan: Thank you for betting on this book and getting it on bookshelves.

Moriah Sunde, Rachael Kincaid, Ashley Wifey, Lindsey Kubly, Erin Carroll, Meg Prellwitz, and Laura Arbo: You beautiful gals are the best team we could ever ask for. You have walked with us through wild dreams and freely given us so much grace as we found our footing these past few years. We've learned from you about love and just how mighty God can be in women. Thank you.

To all the women of The Influence Network: Thank you for being our people. We love you so much and absolutely believe you have influence right where you are. You are ambassadors and blessings and our sisters.

Notes

1. Cited in D. H. Bracey, "The Juvenile Prostitute: Victim and Offender, *Victimology* 8 (1983): 151–60; see Treasures Ministries, "Statistics," http://iamatreasure.com/about-us/statistics/#_edn13 (accessed November 5, 2015).

2. Cited in Bernadette Barton, *Stripped: Inside the Lives of Exotic Dancers* (New York: NYU Press, 2006), xi–xii; see Treasures Ministries, "Statistics," http://iamatreasure.com/about-us/statistics/#_edn13 (accessed November 5, 2015).

3. See Families Civil Liberties Union, "Parentless Statistics," www.fclu.org/parentless-statistics/ U.S. D.H.H.S., Bureau of the Census (accessed November 5, 2015).

4. Ibid.

5. Ibid.

6. HELPS Word-studies, s.v. *"praus,"* BibleHub.com, http://biblehub.com/greek/4239.htm (accessed November 5, 2015).

7. Ellie Holcomb, "I Want to Be Free," on *As Sure As the Sun*, Full Heart Music, 2013. Used by permission.

8. Miles Stanford, *The Complete Green Letters* (Grand Rapids: Zondervan, 1975), 83.

9. Michael Farren and Lauren Daigle, "Come Alive (Dry Bones)," © CentricSongs (admin. by Music Services) / Wordspring Music (admin. by Warner Chappell Music) / Farren Love and War Publishing (admin. by Wordspring Music c/o Warner Chappell Music). All rights reserved. SESAC. Used by permission.

10. John Piper, "For Freedom Christ Has Set Us Free," DesiringGod.org, www.desiringgod.org/sermons/for-freedom-christ-has-set-us-free (accessed November 5, 2015).

11. Krista Tippett, "Transcript for Brené Brown—The Courage to Be Vulnerable," *On Being*, November 21, 2012, www.onbeing.org/program/transcript/4932 (accessed November 12, 2015).

12. Marion Taylor and Heather Lehr Wagner, *Harriet Tubman: Antislavery Activist* (Philadelphia: Chelsea House, 2009), 29.

13. Ibid., 31.

14. Ibid., 38.